THE ROAD TO COURAGEOUS LIVING

LEARNING AUDACIOUS SELF-LOVE AND THE SKILLS TO HARNESS PERSONAL SUCCESS

MICHELLE BURLEIGH

The Road to Courageous Living: Learning Audacious Self-Love and the Skills to Harness Personal Success by Michelle Burleigh

Published by Michelle Burleigh

Visit the author's website at www.soyouvegotcancer.ca

Cover by Virago DSigns, www.viragodsigns.com

Copy editing by Jennifer McIntyre, www.jenmceditor.com, & Leigh Carter

Author Photo by Lisa Poshni Photography

For information about special discounts available for bulk purchases, sales promotions, fund-raising, and speaking engagements, contact Michelle Burleigh at Michelle_Burleigh@hotmail.com.

Print ISBN: 978-1-7386942-0-4

Ebook ISBN: 978-1-7386942-1-1

Printed in Canada

First Edition

CONTENTS

Dedicated to everyone doing the hard work to make a better life for themselves and their families.

PREFACE

I was thirty years old when Katherine walked into the office that day. She was a powerful, stern woman. She was slight in stature but had worked her way up the corporate ladder into a senior leadership position within the organization where we both worked. Katherine was a respected leader. I had always felt intimidated by her until *that* day.

I had heard she was sick, but we were not close enough for me to reach out and see how she was doing. For some reason, I thought it would come off as insincere. It had been months since I had seen her at work. Then one day she walked into the office and right past my desk. It was startlingly clear the toll the chemotherapy and radiation had taken on her. She was gaunt, smaller than usual, and wearing a headwrap that was mostly hidden by her hat. A mere shadow of who she had been. Katherine was 40 years old, and she was losing her battle against brain cancer. My first thought when I saw her was, "What is she doing here? Should she not be resting at home? Why in the hell would she want to be here while she is going through that?!"

As I turned my attention back to my task, I had a fleeting, final thought before moving on with my day: "That will never happen to me."

Years later, however, as I sat in the passenger seat of my partner's car on the way to Juravinski Cancer Centre to be admitted for immediate treatment, I found myself calling my boss to insist he continue sending me work. I still had no idea of what was truly ahead of us, but I now understood why Katherine had still been so fiercely committed to her job even though she was so obviously unwell. Once upon a time, I had been confident I would never find myself in the same position she had been in all those years ago. Now, the harsh reality of life had reared its sometimes-ugly head and forced me to acknowledge that no matter how confident we are in the direction our lives are going, in our own futures—our own fates—ultimately, life is not predictable. At times it can take scary U-turns.

I had to ask myself why, at a time when my entire life had been rocked by the news that I had cancer, I was so insistent on working. What would make a person so determined to please their employer at a time when they could not be certain whether they would ever get to go back to work at all? I cannot speak for Katherine, but I can tell you that for me, it was complete and utter desperation. It was a profound desire to hold on to life when the chances of my continued existence were grim.

It was *panic*.

Luckily for me, despite those unfavorable odds, I lived to tell the tale. Between those days of uncertainty and now, I have had the opportunity to ask myself an abundance of questions about my life —why I made the decisions I did, why I often felt anxious, unhappy and even angry before I got sick, and, most importantly, who I wanted to be going forward. I realized that I wanted to be different than who I had been. For the first time since the world had taught me who the "acceptable" version of me was, I began honoring myself. I began the vicious pursuit of discovering and living the truest version of who I am. Doing so took a level of courage I was not previously able to access, but that does not mean it did not exist. So why did it take coming to the brink of death to unlock my potential?

This book is for anyone who is living or has lived feeling like something is missing, or feels that they may be deceiving themselves and wants to live differently. Life will never be perfect. Making courageous decisions is rarely easy, but when we free ourselves from the expectations we believe the world has of us, from the expectations we have of ourselves, and from all our self-limiting beliefs, we can learn to make decisions that bring us true happiness, true satisfaction, true fulfillment. If that means being a freelance artist who travels the world, is happy with their own company and never has a 9-to-5 job, then so be it. If that means being married, having two kids and a white picket fence and working that 9-to-5 corporate job, then so be it. Whoever it is that you want to be and however you want to live your life is your own choice. The important part is that you feel happy, satisfied, and fulfilled. Whatever you choose to do, you must do it because it's what you want to do, not because it's what you've been told you should do.

Resolving to live our truth is merely the start of our journey to authenticity. It does not happen overnight. In my case, I believe the work will go on for all my remaining days, but I still wonder about the speed at which change might happen if we didn't limit our thoughts about what is possible. We intentionally avoid change because we get stuck in the comfort of familiarity, or because our subconscious minds protect us from past trauma. Sometimes we get stuck just because we know change will be hard, or because we don't believe in ourselves enough to effect a different result.

Though I know I will never have the answer, I still ponder how much progress we could make if we just accepted it will be hard and sometimes painful, and commit to it anyway.

When we choose to live our lives authentically and with absolute vulnerability, there is nothing the world can take away from us. It just takes a little bit of courage and an effective strategy to get started. If you want to lay your head down at night knowing you are living to the fullest, this book will give you some strategies to get the ball rolling. My hope for you is that you enjoy reading about my journey of learning audacious self-love, take away a few nuggets for consideration, and learn new ways to make more courageous decisions in your own life.

CHAPTER ONE
FAMILY

For as long as I can remember, every year as we approached the Christmas season, my grandmother could be found in her kitchen, overflowing with baking ingredients and the aromas of some sort of deliciousness in the oven. I loved to visit her before her famous baking baskets were ready for delivery to friends and family because it meant I could sneak a treat here and there. I loved my grandmother's baking. As my brother and I got older, we could request goodies for our own baskets, and without fail, Grandma would make them for us.

Christmas dinner was always at her apartment in Toronto. I was a preteen when she got remarried, and as much as she loved to bake, her new husband loved to cook. So he made the dinner, and she made the desserts that everyone indulged in as we sat together at her tiny dining room table. Every year, we would also get to bring a goodie basket home with us. No surprise—the treats never lasted more than a week.

2017 was a special year, unlike any year our family had previously experienced. Grandma was eighty years old and had recently become a cancer survivor. It was time for her to pass the baking torch. My then-boyfriend, Marvin, and I had bought our first house together a year earlier, and we had brought our children together to make a blended family of four—my biological daughter, Victoria, and Marvin's biological daughter, Isabelle. Only three weeks apart in age, they became playmates quickly. We were eager to establish our own family traditions. I was excited that the girls were eager to help me in the kitchen. And so, it made the most sense for the girls and me to relieve Grandma of her decades-old tradition and take over in our new home with our new family.

My thirty-seventh birthday was also coming up that year. I had spent the vast majority of my adult life looking for the right partner who could help me build a peaceful, loving home filled with people who would revel in such family activities. It made me feel warm and fuzzy inside to have my dreams actualized. Family meant everything to me.

It was November, and we were running out of time to complete the traditional baking baskets. We aimed to deliver them no later than the second week of December. We still had a lot to do, so we rallied the troops. My mom and grandmother joined one of my daughters, Victoria, and me to get the rest done. It took us a couple of hours, some hard work and some not-so-hard work, to complete the day's to-do list. My mom and Victoria joked and made silly faces as they cut out the cookies and decorated them on the pan. My grandmother looked on as she stirred the melting marshmallows at the stove, and I shook my head with a disapproving look as Mom and Victoria made a mess with candy sprinkles, even though there was no one else I would rather have been with in that moment.

We were almost done cleaning up. Grandma had already tapped out and gone home. Suddenly, a sharp, pounding pain assaulted my brain, and my peripheral vision started to darken. I stood holding the kitchen counter, waiting for it to pass. It was the third time this week. I had never experienced a migraine before having my daughter, Victoria. Within months of giving birth to her, I had two, but nothing in the four years since then. And now three in a row. It was excruciating, and a little scary, because the pain was debilitating, but as many other mothers of tiny humans would agree, no matter how bad we feel, the show must go on.

I could not figure out why they had suddenly come on again. It was also curious, because these headaches were somewhat different than the early post-birth migraines. They came on hard and fast, but if I sat or lay down, they would subside quickly. I could not make sense of it. However, my birthday and the holidays were coming up fast, and I did not have time to ponder the root cause of the mystery headaches. So, I did what so many other people would do in that situation: I thanked my mom and saw her out, I lay down for five minutes, and when the pain subsided enough, I got back up and finished the job.

CHAPTER TWO

THE MYSTERY INJURY

I have always hated running, and the bikes at the gym never feel like enough of a workout—unless they are part of a spin class. The ellipticals always felt like a good balance between intensity and low-impact activity, so mostly I used those. It was a Saturday morning, and I was working out on the elliptical at the gym. I was utterly wiped out after the week and not thrilled to be there, but exercise was non-negotiable in my life, so it just needed to be done, no matter how tired I was. Moreover, Christmas was coming, which meant I would shamelessly enjoy an abundance of baked goods. That day, my daughter Isabelle and I were planning on spending the afternoon baking. So I carried on, finished my workout, and headed home.

Isabelle was so excited to decorate the cookies. She has always enjoyed baking and is a great helper. At only five years old, she had more focus and determination than I had had for most of my life! I was grateful for her help and overjoyed by the smile on her face. But after a long day of activity, my back was sore. That in itself was not unusual, as I had suffered lower back issues most of my life. But as I finished cleaning up the kitchen counters, I felt more inclined to climb onto them and take a nap than to move on to the next task. While I did not climb on the counter, I did pause for the day for some much-needed rest.

"Babe, I need to sit down," I told Marvin the next day. "I don't know what's up with my back, but I just cannot stand up straight."

Earlier that morning, much as I did not want to get out of bed, I needed to go and renew my passport. But when I woke up and tried to sit up and swing my legs over the side of the bed, something pinched, and I immediately lay back down. After taking a deep breath, I rolled off the side of the bed like a solider navigating hostile terrain. We had not booked a trip just yet, but Marvin and I desperately needed a break from everyday life and were trying to find a hideaway for a week in the Bahamas. There is nothing worse than wanting to take a trip and realizing your passport is expired.

So I pushed through. I had had my new photos taken at the small shop in the local mall, and then Marvin and I walked through the mall's center to wait for them to be processed. Walking was painful for me, so we stopped at the armchairs in the center of the mall.

Flare-ups in my back were not unusual, but they were typically a result of me doing something outrageous, like tobogganing down a ski hill or dancing in heels all night long. Or that time years ago when I'd painted my three-story townhouse from top to bottom in a week. It was a lousy idea, and I'd ended up with back pain for nine months. Over the next few years, my back pain had lessened as I had consistently been strength training to manage the problem. As a result, it had been quite some time since it had felt this poorly. I had not done anything to warrant this pain. Between the gym and baking the day before, I was tired at the end of the day, but I should have woken up feeling refreshed. Yet there I was, unable to stand up straight, unable to sit down comfortably, and it was getting worse by the minute.

By that night, I could barely move. The pain had escalated to nearly unbearable. I had to return to work the next day, and I knew that was unrealistic: the pain was strong enough to knock out my ability to even think clearly. Reluctantly, I admitted it was time for a trip to the hospital.

A few hours later, I returned with two prescription medications and a diagnosis of "locked muscle." I was unsure why a muscle would lock from a typical workout, but I was nearly hysterical by that point and just needed relief. An hour later, I gently rocked in my big fluffy rocking chair, comfortably numb, not caring that I might be drooling on myself a little thanks to the hydromorphone the doctor had given me. It was as though the pain had been instantly muted, or maybe the drugs just made me care a whole lot less about it than before. Either way, I was finally able to rest.

Two days later, I had not returned to work, nor had the muscle released. The medication made me light-headed, so I spent most of my time resting in my rocking chair. Even if my mind was clear enough to drive, the thought of sitting at the office all day or commuting in the car was anxiety-producing. I needed to get back to managing my life, though, which was impossible as long as I was taking that medication. Between the waning of one dose and the fresh rush of warmth caused by the next, I decided to book an appointment with my family doctor for a second opinion.

The irony of living in a small town with an aging population is that there are a plethora of doctors in town, yet many of them do not take new patients. Finding a new family doctor had not been an urgent need until only a few weeks earlier when Victoria needed booster shots. Marvin already had a trusted doctor who also wasn't accepting new patients. I had searched online for doctors and made calls to numerous medical offices, only to be told time and again that their doctors were not accepting new patients. I learned quickly that, in a small town, the best way to find things is to ask around, so that's what I did.

The doctor I ultimately picked did not come highly recommended. However, she was close to home and accepting new patients, so we chose her, even if only temporarily. After our first encounter, I felt like my being in her office was an inconvenience. It had been clear this would not be a long-term relationship. But on that day, when my muscle was still on fire and I needed a second opinion, she was convenient to access, which is a privilege not all Canadians have.

After a short discussion, the doctor concluded it was indeed a locked muscle and switched the pain medication from hydromorphone, a narcotic, to meloxicam, a nonsteroidal anti-inflammatory drug (NSAID). With most of the work week behind me, I decided to continue using the heavy-hitting hydromorphone in hopes it would help the still-locked muscle to release. I resolved to switch to the NSAID by Sunday so I could safely return to work.

The weekend came and went, but the muscle remained locked. As planned, I took the final dose of the narcotic on Sunday morning and then switched to the meloxicam. I needed to clear my head and get back to work. There were dollars to make and university educations to prepare for!

But all that day, I couldn't silence the uneasy, nagging voice at the back of my head: it was odd that, days after hurting myself, I still needed such strong medication to manage the pain and that the muscle was still locked. But neither the emergency room doctor nor my family doctor seemed concerned, so, since I am no medical professional, I reluctantly accepted their advice. In the meantime, to help myself, I booked a massage appointment with a registered massage therapist and mentally prepared myself to return to work.

I GOT UP ON MONDAY MORNING AND MOVED FORWARD with life, albeit hobbling like Hoggle in the children's movie *The Labyrinth*, freshly treated with the new medication.

"I realize I am wearing leggings and Uggs," I told my boss when I finally returned to work, "but I am still struggling with this injury, and I could not wear something more restrictive. I am really sorry about that."

"That's okay. Do what you need to do, Michelle. We are just happy to have you back," was the somewhat unsurprising response. I had been gone for a whole week. I did not feel much better than I had during my week off but at least I could finally walk again.

I had been working for this employer for over three years and had come to truly appreciate them. After working in the trenches and enduring unacceptable behaviour and conditions with my previous employers, this one had proven to be more interested in what I could contribute to the organization than what I wore to work. I will admit that coming from an employer of ten years with something to say about every little thing to this one, who barely batted an eye at a peeking midriff, was an adjustment. Even three years later, I had difficulty walking into the office in casual shoes, no matter how necessary. But at last, I had started coming out of the staunch corporate fog and genuinely appreciated working for an employer who valued my contributions over my appearance. Why, earlier that year, I had even gotten up the courage to visit my hairdresser for a haircut and a beautiful balayage lilac dye job, just for fun. When I arrived at work the following morning, I was very nervous about how my new look would be received. Like a rescue dog, I cautiously accepted the compliments from my colleagues, but waited to be reprimanded. That time never came.

I HAD ONLY BEEN BACK TO WORK FOR ONE DAY WHEN things began to take a troubling turn, and I called my doctor back.

"Hello, this is Michelle Burleigh calling. I was in to see the doctor last week. She prescribed a couple of medications. I started taking them on Sunday night, and I have started bruising. There are two of them on my leg. They are greenish-blue and look like paint splatters. I think it might be one of the medications. Can I speak with the doctor about it?"

"I will speak with the doctor and get back to you shortly," replied the office manager.

"Thank you."

FOUR HOURS LATER, MY PHONE RANG. THE DOCTOR'S office was calling back. "The doctor wanted me to let you know that the bruising is likely not due to your medications. However, call us back if they get worse or do not improve. Also, you should call the pharmacy if you have any questions about the medications."

I did not quite understand why I would need to call the pharmacy to ask about side effects of a medication my doctor had just prescribed. I had always been able to talk to my former family doctor if I had concerns. I suppose it made sense, given how busy doctors are, generally, but this was new, and I was confused. I did not question the woman's instructions. Instead, I said thank you and hung up the phone.

That night, I studied the bruises on my leg. They did not appear worse, but they did not seem better, either. I stood straight and turned slowly in the mirror, curious about whether there were any other mystery bruises. As the back of my shoulder came into view, I noticed another one. It was hard to tell, but there appeared to be another one on my arm, though it was faint. Had I not seen those the night before? Were they new?

The following morning, I noticed a tender spot on the outer side of my right thigh. It was not uncommon for me to run into things, so finding tender bruises was not unheard of. However, upon inspection, I felt panic reverberate through my body. This bruise was big, about the size of an egg. It was dark green, and in the middle of the bruise, it looked like the blood vessel below the skin had exploded. It was puffy and sore.

It had been nearly two weeks since my injury from the gym. I was tired. I was tired of being in pain. Hell, I was tired of being tired. I had even gotten two massages earlier that week to work out the persistent aches, but they did not relieve the constant throbbing in my hip. I was beginning to feel like I was not getting the support I needed from the healthcare professionals I had spoken to. When I called the doctor's office back the following day, I was not as calm as the first time I had called.

"Well, it seems the doctor was wrong," I began. "It IS the medication. I now have bruises all over, and I stopped taking the medication yesterday, but bruises keep popping up. Last night I read the information page that came with the prescriptions. Under *Side Effects*, it says, '**If you are experiencing these severe side effects, call your doctor immediately—unusual bleeding, unusual**

bruising ...' but I did that, and you told me it probably was *not* the medication. There is a BIG problem here, and I need to talk to the doctor."

I will admit, it was not my finest moment.

"I do not appreciate your tone, Ms. Burleigh," the nurse replied coldly. "If you are so concerned, you should have just booked an appointment. Doctors are not trained to know medication side effects, so you should have called the pharmacy as we told you to do. Now, we have an appointment available at four-thirty p.m. today. Do you want the appointment?"

My anger grew.

"When patients call with serious concerns," I retorted, disregarding her question, "whether the doctor is trained in side effects or not, maybe the least she could have done is understand what the issue is in the first place because I'm pretty sure this is not normal, and the pamphlet says the same thing. And I do not appreciate *your* tone! No, I do <u>not</u> want your appointment!"

As soon as my handset crashed down into its cradle, I apologized to it. A split second later, my cubicle neighbor popped his head over the wall, wide-eyed and grinning at the early-morning drama in the office.

"You okay?" he asked.

I nodded at him politely, but I was seeing red. I did not understand why I was the only one who was concerned. It was nearly impossible to ignore the bruises or what might be causing them. So far as I knew, random bruises could only mean one thing. I could no longer deny that I was bleeding internally and assumed that was never a good thing. I could not help but wonder where else I was bleeding that I could not see. Was I overreacting? Was I being dramatic? I questioned myself. Maybe I was being paranoid. *It must just be me.*

So, I did what seemed logical. I worked out the day as my employment contract expected me to do. At the end of the workday, I left the office looking like I had stood in front of a Sgt. Splatter firing squad. Bruises and all, I slapped a smile on my face and went to the holiday gathering at Victoria's school like a responsible parent, just as I had worked the day like a responsible employee.

Later that evening, I was standing in the doorway of my daughter's Montessori school. Children, parents, and teachers were milling about, chatting, and laughing. I did not feel as social as usual. Still, it was an exciting event, and I would not allow myself to miss another celebratory event ahead of Christmas. I had already missed my favorite event of the season, the office holiday party. My employer was known throughout our industry for throwing fantastic parties, and we employees looked forward to them all year. If there was one thing you could count on us for, it was that we worked hard and we played harder. No, I would not miss another special event—especially not one that was so meaningful to Victoria. As a social, outgoing ambivert, I needed the human connection, and the women who ran the school were some of the most incredible humans I had ever met. I always left them feeling like my cup was a little fuller than when I'd arrived. So, despite feeling awful, I needed to be there to support my daughter and her school.

The night was not about me. It did not matter how terrible I felt. I had already spent weeks dealing with a pesky locked muscle, which had my entire family and me in a perpetual state of misery. Tonight was about Victoria's school holiday social.

Her school always did such a fantastic job of putting on a get-together. The staff's love of the kids and their creativity made these occasions magical, time and again. Unlike my own elementary school experience of piling hundreds of people into a gymnasium for holiday celebrations, these gatherings were always more intimate. We made up our own little community, and it was beautiful to be a part of it. There was a unique camaraderie between the families. The twenty or so junior kindergarteners, who made up a third of the entire school's population, surrounded their music teacher, who sat at the electronic piano in the corner of their cozy classroom as the kids prepared to deliver the musical performance they had practised so diligently. It was a special occasion, indeed. Marvin and our other daughter, Isabelle, were in attendance, along with my grandmother, who rarely had the opportunity to celebrate such occasions with us.

As much as I wanted to be excited, to be present in the moment—Victoria surely deserved it—I could not get there. I was tired beyond belief. I was also miserable. Earlier that day, I'd had a meeting at work with a senior executive about some help they were looking for on an upcoming project. I am not tolerant of workplace politics to begin with, and the team on this particular initiative had a complicated working relationship.

"So tell me," I'd asked the exec, "what am I in for with this group?"

He seemed taken back by my question, chuckled, and proceeded in the only way I had ever seen him conduct business: with utter diplomacy and professionalism.

I struggled through that meeting and the rest of the day. With my approaching birthday, I sensed that my body was changing in unusual ways, and it was playing on my mind. As a dedicated careerwoman and mom, I did not have time to feel unwell. So, I smiled as the first stroke of the piano queued up the kids, and when no one was looking, I snuck to the back of the room, hidden away from the crowd, and sat down on the floor to recharge enough for dinner after the show.

It turned out my brave smile wasn't fooling everyone. At the end of the show, one of the teachers, a warm and caring woman named Mrs. Siobhan, came up to me with a concerned look on her face.

"Michelle, you don't look well," she said quietly. "Are you feeling okay?"

"I am fine—just a little tired. I think it is the Christmas break coming up. It is just so busy, and I cannot seem to get ahead of the tiredness."

"Well, take it easy. I hope you feel better soon." Mrs. Siobhan did not look like she was buying it, but she left it at that.

"I will. Thanks."

We all bundled up into our coats and hats and boots and the crowd began to file out the door. Mrs. Siobhan gave us all big hugs, and as our family walked out the door, she handed the girls a bag of reindeer food, telling them to make sure to put it out the night before Christmas so the reindeer could have a bite to eat, too, and we left.

"So, do you think it's time to go to the hospital?" Marvin said as we drove to the local diner.

Marvin is the strong, silent type. I will admit that his question was startling. Like too many men, he hardly ever went to the doctor and hadn't visited one in the two years we had been together. So, the suggestion was unnerving. As quickly as the panic hit me, I shoved it back down. There was no time for hospital visits. I would be fine.

CHAPTER THREE
THE DIAGNOSIS

The morning after Victoria's Christmas party, and after nearly two weeks of constant pain, the effort to get out of bed was akin to climbing the Everest summit—with no training and a strictly fast-food diet. Yet, I had already missed a whole week of work and could not convince myself to lie back down. My office tea mug with the quote "Can't stop, won't stop" was a constant reminder of my work ethic, and I needed to get my head back in the game.

Other than Marvin, no one seemed concerned about the muscle that was not healing in my hip or the bruises that had mysteriously popped up. As much as I wanted to be unconcerned too, I was having trouble ignoring the nagging sense of worry in the back of my brain. But stubbornness won out: this pain had prevented me from doing life for too long, and I was fed up with it. And more to the point, if I were to call in sick again, could I justify another day off?

I pictured myself calling in and saying something like, "Hi, boss. So, I feel pretty terrible, and there appears to be no good medical reason for it, but I decided to take another day off anyway. So, see you when I see you!" I could just imagine his face. I knew the whole scenario sounded ridiculous, of course, but even so, I could not convince my body to get out of bed and stand up. I needed someone to confirm there was a good reason to stay home again. I could not lose my job. We had just bought our first home. We had financial commitments, and I had worked too damn hard just to get fired. The only option I could think of, short of going to the emergency department again, which seemed equally ridiculous, was to call TeleHealth Ontario. That is the telephone healthcare service offered by the Ontario government that allows callers to speak with a registered nurse about medical issues 24/7. I had used it many times in the past for both my own issues and my children's symptoms and illnesses.

But I was still hesitant to call them. The tone of the conversations with health care professionals over the last few days had me feeling like I was overreacting, whining. I had gone from feeling serious concern over my symptoms to feeling foolish for even contemplating picking up the phone to talk with a nurse. But still, that nagging voice in my head told me to dial the number. Lucky for me, it was not a busy morning, and I was immediately connected with a nurse.

She listened to my descriptions, asked a few more questions, and then said, "Ms. Burleigh, based on what you shared with me this morning, we recommend going to your local emergency department immediately. We will send a copy of this assessment to the hospital, so they have these details when you get there."

A little stunned, I replied, "Sure. I can drop my daughter off at school and head to the hospital."

"Ms. Burleigh, we do not recommend driving. If you would like, I can call an ambulance for you."

Whoa! That's a little overboard. Why the heck do I need an ambulance?!

"Thank you for the offer. I will get myself to the hospital immediately."

Though her reaction seemed overly cautious, I appreciated the advice and her concern. It was nice to feel like a medical professional was taking me seriously for a change. After dropping my daughter off at school, I drove straight to the hospital. Luckily, it was only about ten minutes away from home. As I walked into the emergency department, I was still confused by the recommendation not to operate a vehicle, but it wouldn't be long before I understood why.

Score! The ER was practically empty—almost unheard-of in Ontario—so the wait for triage would not be long. Maybe I could still make it to work this morning.

I walked straight into Registration and Triage, where the triage nurse asked, "The reason for your visit today?"

"I am here because I hurt my hip. My doctor gave me a couple of medications for it and now I am bruising, my blood vessels are bursting, and I am hemorrhaging."

Without missing a beat and with barely a look, she replied, "The doctor is just going to tell you to stop taking the medications."

"I already did that, and I am still bruising," I responded.

"So, you are here for heavy menstruation?"

I stared at her, aghast. We were officially going down a rabbit hole.

"No," I said, trying to hold on to my patience. "Am I bleeding? Yes, but I shouldn't be bleeding like this. I am here because my body looks like something from a crime scene investigation, and I do not know why. I called TeleHealth, and they told me to drop what I was doing and come here."

"Right. We call TeleHealth '1-800-GO-TO-EMERG' around here," she said flippantly.

My last remaining atom of patience left my body. "I do not care what you call TeleHealth. I need to see a doctor, NOW."

She casually said, "Well, we are not terribly busy here this morning, so I guess we can take a couple of vials of blood to see what is going on."

If I had tried, I could not have mustered more sarcasm for the "Thanks" I shot at her after her generous offer.

I remained in the public washroom for the duration of my wait. My condition would not allow me to stray too far. When I heard a nurse call my name in the waiting room, I rushed to wash my hands and meet her.

By the time I got back to the waiting room, she was already gone. I picked up the phone on the wall beside the locked double doors, and it rang without me pressing any buttons. A nurse picked up and said, "Yes?"

"Oh, hi. Someone just called my name. I'm here now."

A few seconds later, a nurse stepped through the automatic double doors, clearly unimpressed that she had to come out a second time for me. I tried to thank her for her patience, but she ignored me as she walked four paces ahead of me. *Friendly place*, I thought wryly, as I hurried along behind her. She waved her arm into a room, indicating that I should enter it and wait for the doctor.

The doctor arrived soon afterwards, asked a few questions about the reason for my visit, and then ordered the bloodwork the triage nurse had predicted. I silently thanked the powers that be for the doctor's kind demeanor.

An hour later, the doctor returned to the room, a puzzled look on her face. "Something looks funny in your blood," she said, looking at the chart in her hand. "You have almost no platelets."

"What does that mean?"

"Well, it could be something as simple as your spleen eating them up, or it could be cancer."

I was beginning to feel like these folks needed a lesson on bedside manners. However, that was not the first time a doctor had dropped the C-word on me. As sure as I was that the strep throat I had developed six years ago was not throat cancer, I was sure this was not cancer, either.

I thought, *Man, I really hope it's not my spleen. I do not want a scar on my chest—I want to wear a strapless wedding dress some day!*

"We will need to send your blood to another hospital more equipped for this kind of diagnostic testing."

"Okay. I live around the corner. Can I go home and have lunch, watch the news for a bit and come back?"

"That is probably not a good idea. We have a Tim Horton's in the building. Why don't you get yourself a coffee and something to eat. I will have someone bring you a warm blanket."

Fine, I thought. A few minutes later I sat on the hospital bed with a tea and a bagel. I was beyond tired. I had been living a life of perpetual exhaustion for weeks and would have loved to catch some Zs, but sleeping in a hospital is nearly impossible. Alas, life did not often present the opportunity to rest guilt-free, so I finished up my meal and snuggled up with the warm blanket. I almost made it to dreamland when the doctor came back into the room.

"Do you want to have someone here to talk about this?" she said without preamble.

What? "No need."

"How old are your kids?" the doctor asked.

Oh no. "It is the worst-case scenario, isn't it?"

"Is there someone who can get your kids after school?"

What?! "Why?"

"I'm sorry to tell you this, but you have leukemia. You need to leave here and go to a cancer center to start treatment immediately. Would you rather go to Princess Margaret Cancer Centre in Toronto or Juravinski Cancer Centre in Hamilton?"

WHAT?! I could not find words. How could I possibly respond to that? It felt like an explosion in my brain, and a moment later, my first thought formed:

People do not come back from leukemia. I am going to die.

Two hours later, Marvin and I walked through Juravinski Cancer Centre, stepped onto the elevator and pressed the fourth-floor button. "Going up," said the tinny elevator voice. My first thought was that this was far too chipper a voice to use for people entering a cancer ward. Having the doors open to the hematology unit was surreal. It felt like I was watching a scary movie from the first-person perspective. I should have been sitting on my couch at home, wrapped in a blanket, surrounded by my family. But my legs deceived me by moving forward, propelling me off the elevator and through the halls. Maybe it was a dream? The next thing I knew, I was sitting in a hospital bed hooked up to three IV lines. The nurse asked me to sign waivers releasing the hospital of any legal responsibility if I contracted a disease from the blood products about to flow into my veins.

The nurse was a permanent fixture in the room—checking my blood pressure, temperature, and eyes (which I later learned would indicate whether there was bleeding in my brain). I watched, bewildered, as control of my life slipped away, and I involuntarily handed my fate to complete strangers. But under that hazy feeling, I was angry. All I had ever tried to do with my life was simply to be a good person and do better. To educate myself as best I could, to work hard to ensure financial security for my family and me, and to have an easier life than my parents ever had. And yet, at every turn, it felt like I was getting punched in the face. Why was it so damn hard?

I had spent the last fifteen years working in corporate business—the first in my family lineage to have such a career. I had watched people, some younger than I, excel in business, buy their first houses, and take exotic trips in those early years. I wanted that too. I wanted to come home from wild vacations with exciting stories to tell. I wanted to have money in the bank and beautiful cars. But it felt like I was constantly climbing a sandy hill, every step up barely a step forward. But as I sat there in the bed watching the flurry of activity around me—*for* me—the shimmering illusion of the things that seemed important melted away. And I thought, *this is total bullshit*.

I had worked hard my whole life to achieve those things I thought I wanted, only to be sitting in this bed about to die, and I had still not made it to Bora Bora. I asked myself, was it worth all those times I had run myself into the ground to pursue those things? I had somehow convinced myself that power and money would make things better. That I could—should—achieve *all* the things, and then I could rest easy. I had believed that acquiring material things would validate that I had won—but won at what? As I watched the nurse put on gloves before popping the biohazardous oral chemotherapy drugs out of their individually wrapped packaging, I thought, what a crock! Because at that moment, no amount of status, power, or money would save my life, and if I did die here, as my failing liver and increasing temperature suggested might very well happen, the only thing I could have taken with me was my memories. I was furious!

I said to the nurse beside me, "You know, I think I'm going to quit my job, write a book and do some public speaking. Other people need to know that the world is lying to them."

She barely skipped a beat as she turned to look at me, "That sounds like a great idea. But how about we get through today first?"

Fair point.

"HELLO, MICHELLE. WE HAVE THE RESULTS OF YOUR first bone marrow biopsy."

Marvin, my dad, and I huddled around the newest member of my medical team to find out what we were dealing with and what was to come.

I said, "Okay, Doc, what are we dealing with?"

"It is a good thing you came in when you did. Your bone marrow is composed of ninety percent leukemia cells. Had you not come in when you did, you likely would have experienced a brain bleed that would have ended your life. Likely by tomorrow.

"You have acute promyelocytic leukemia," he continued, "in the high-risk category. If not the rarest, it's close to the rarest you can have. The good news is you have an eighty-five to ninety percent chance of a full recovery. It would have been ninety to ninety-five percent if you were at low to moderate risk, but the concentration of leukemic cells is too high. There is a good chance you will be cured as long as you make it through the next ten days."

My jaw hung open. Emotions immediately flooded through me. The most powerful one was anger. I was furious that we had wasted so much time looking for the answer to the mystery bruises. How much worse was this going to be because we had not caught it sooner? "What does that mean," I demanded, "that I need to make it through the next ten days?!"

He completely ignored my question and moved on. "There are four phases of treatment—the first is Induction, which will start tomorrow and continue for thirty-six days. You can expect to be here for the duration. After that, Consolidation One will be thirty consecutive days, Consolidation Two will be thirty days spanning six weeks, and Maintenance will be two years.

"You should have someone bring you some of your personal belongings. Also, the food here is terrible. We used to have an in-house chef who was quite good, but he is no longer here, thanks to healthcare cuts. So, see if someone can bring you food too."

Dumbfounded, I sat and stared at him, my head spinning.

CHAPTER FOUR

GRAPPLING WITH REALITY

The idea of being unwell, unavailable, and unable to parent my children during such a critical time in their young lives made me feel utter despair. At only five years old, they were still in the formative years of their lives, where modelled behaviours count the most.

And why had the doctor not answered my question about the ten days? What I had just learned was inconceivable no matter how I tried to process it. It was altogether too much at once.

The emotions bubbled up over the edge and paralyzed me. The illusion of control I had worked so hard to maintain all these years had just slipped away. Having experienced the struggle of getting someone, *anyone*, to take me seriously about my condition made it extremely difficult to trust this doctor who had quite abruptly just walked into my life. In retrospect, I realize I should have been grateful for his help, considering he was the man tasked with literally saving my life. Still, my experience leading up to this moment made it very difficult to accept that anyone but me was going to save me—and worse, I knew that was an impossibility.

In the moment, I was beyond angry. Angry at myself and angry at the world. Throughout much of my young adulthood, I had always let life happen to me. I knew the direction I wanted to move in but had never set a plan. It is no wonder that every time I came to a juncture in life, be it a job or a relationship, I accepted it as a forward step. I rarely asked myself if something or someone was right for me. Instead, I graciously accepted the company of others and took comfort in having a steady income. The idea of critical thought—about what was important to me, or what I wanted for my future—was not much of a consideration. I had always wanted all the fun things but my prime directive had always been financial security at all costs. After all, when I was growing up, thinking critically was not how children's movies taught young girls to achieve happiness. Eventually, Prince Charming would swoop in, and everything would be perfect and effortless. We would live happily ever after, hopefully with fewer chirping birds first thing in the morning.

I was missing guardrails to guide me through life. While there were undoubtedly occasions when I drew the line, the circumstances were often extreme—and few and far between. And so, I continued to move forward but had come to feel like the little silver ball in a pinball machine. I took a step forward at each juncture, but eventually, my choices taught me to expect a step or two back. It took many years to recognize that this was not a healthy pattern for more reasons than one. To begin with, life is not about reaching a destination. If we brace ourselves and barrel through life, we will miss all the good between the start and the finish line. And I had recently become acutely aware that, sometimes, we never make it to our preferred finish line.

But also, each time we make a misstep, requiring us to course correct, we end up with another scar. I was furious at myself for blindly allowing this to happen to me. Despite all the barreling through I had done and all the scars I had accumulated, I had landed right here, sitting in front of a doctor telling me I might die. I felt like I had not reached my pot of gold yet. Heck, I hadn't even learned out to enjoy the journey yet. I was angry that despite being hyper-focused on succeeding and trying my best to be a good human, this is where it had got me: in a hospital bed, unsure if I would ever see my children again. My definition of success was decimated instantly, and I wondered how many other people were living the same way, focusing on things that were not as meaningful as they believed them to be, blithely telling themselves they had all the time in the world to focus on their partner, kids or friends later. Meanwhile, they felt they just had to answer that one email or sit through that one urgent meeting, either through lack of awareness or, worse, because they felt like they had no choice.

I recalled stories of middle-aged senior executives having heart attacks and leaving this earth too soon, or women who were admitted to hospital repeatedly for unexplained gastrointestinal flare-ups, only to be told by a specialist to see a mental health professional. Stories like those happen too frequently, and even in their obituaries, their family, friends and colleagues praise the deceased's work ethic or say that they were always so reliable. How could someone so young, even someone who seemed to follow the general rules of good health, everyone wonders, have a massive heart attack and die?

As I lay there in that bed, the answer was clear. In at least some cases, it was stress. Without understanding how to move through stress, or rather, how to allow stress to move through me, I had often found myself on the other side of life's challenges but more wound up than ever.

When I said to my nurses and doctors, "I think stress contributed to me getting sick," they tended to glaze over and nod their heads.

Some flat-out denied the possibility. The comical irony was that, in the next breath, the same medical professionals would tell me to be sure I eliminated as much stress as possible from my life during treatment.

It took some time to start putting these puzzle pieces together. Eventually, I began to understand why healthcare professionals might react that way. It seemed that, in general, medical professionals who were even willing to consider the link between stress and illness were ridiculed. This was apparent when I, myself, broached the topic with professionals who immediately struck the very idea down. Another thing I notice is that there appears to be a never-ending debate over whether or not we should acknowledge the lifestyle of a cancer patient before their diagnosis. It seems this mentality relates to the undesirability of patients internalizing and shaming themselves for things they did in their lives that may have contributed to illness.

While I could understand that, and believe there is a time and place for such conversations, personally I found it patronizing. I would rather have known how I may have contributed to my condition so that I could fix it if I were allowed the time on this earth to do so. Did I blame myself? No. Would some people? Yes. But should that not be a personal choice—to receive this information and then deal with it as we see fit? I believe so. Are we as humans so obstinate that we cannot be flexible enough to treat someone the way *they* want to be treated?

Since my diagnosis, I have come to believe there is an opportunity to customize a patient's experience by understanding who they are, what their needs might be, and what they want to focus on. If a patient is given the chance to reduce their risk of ending up ill again, can we not assume that at least some people want that opportunity? The answer is a resounding yes. And just as most of us aspire to healthier habits and behaviours, I believe that we are better able to face our health challenges from a position of power and positivity rather than from one of fear and lack of awareness or information. And frankly, the only way to make long-lasting, effective change is to acknowledge our past behaviour.

Regardless of how the nurses looked at me when I brought up the issue of stress, it was clear to me that stress is a major contributing factor to illness. But stress does not typically just *happen*, so what are these people, including myself, so stressed about?

It was not until I suffered a mental breakdown a few months after diagnosis and started picking up the pieces again that I realized we, as a society, are making ourselves sick. How often do we work ourselves into the ground for a promotion or put aside self-care to prioritize the needs of others? We are not taught how to take care of ourselves, how to achieve that work–life balance that is so much in the news lately. Even that term, work-life balance, prioritizes work! We are not taught to manage stress. In fact, men are, by and large, still told to be men—suck it up and do not be emotional. And women ... Well, we are told to be everything to everyone else —a star employee, partner, mother—but if we dare to be anything to ourselves, we are selfish. It is absolutely no wonder that, despite advances in cancer care and the increase in survival rates, more of us are getting cancer and other chronic illnesses. And for the first time in decades, our neighbors to the south, the United States of America, are seeing Americans who are dying younger than their parents and grandparents before them.

Of course, societal expectations are stressing us out and making us sick. What I did not understand in those early days as this knowing began to form, is that we individually make up society. So while I directed my anger outward, spent so much time blaming 'society', it had not yet occurred to me that I was as much to blame for the unmanageable stress as those I pointed my finger at. More on that later.

It is also important to note another growing trend: we live in a society increasingly dominated by absolutes. We are either absolute red or absolute blue. We are absolutely right and they are absolutely wrong. And these entrenched positions are supported and perpetuated by social media. The problem is that reasonable people who tend to live in the logic that exists between extremes do not make it a habit of defending the reasonability of living in that space. They just live it. The louder voices, the squeakier wheels, so to speak, often belong to those who promote ideals and spread lies.

We do not need to live by absolutes. We were born with the incredible ability to make up our own minds, to use judgment, logic and instincts to guide our decision-making. We possess the creativity to pick the dreams and goals that suit our personal interests, and to hell with anyone who does not like it because we are not here to live for others. In the spirit of dispelling absolutes, it is fair to mention here that if living to serve others is our choice, then so be it, but we need to realize that the person most impacted by and responsible for our actions is ourselves. If we make ourselves sick scrambling to meet the expectations of others, it is we, ourselves, who will live the consequences. So, rather than preaching absolutes or taking sides, I would rather be open to the world's possibilities. I prefer to seek to understand; I choose to celebrate the wins of others, and I decide what qualifies as a win for myself. I choose the unabashed pursuit of self-love and happiness, not the ideals of others.

The epiphany was earth-shattering. Enough so that, despite a lifetime of shrinking myself to avoid the spotlight, I knew I had to get my message out: *You matter more than the role you are trying to play*. You cannot take a luxury car to the grave with you, but when you take your last breath, you can do so with wonderful memories of a life well lived. You can die peacefully, sure in the knowledge that you lived an authentic, meaningful life. You do not need to die for your career, a house full of things, or other people's expectations.

Every occasion in my life in which I had abandoned myself suddenly bubbled up with this realization. The times I allowed people to speak to me with utter disrespect, and then forgave them only to have it happen again, or when I made decisions to do things I knew was not right for me but did it anyway because I wanted to prove myself worthy. I thought of my own mother, who has suffered from severe gastrointestinal disease over the years but is praised for being the nicest, most helpful and available person. But how nice, helpful or available is she for herself?

THE DOCTOR NEVER DID ANSWER MY QUESTION ABOUT making it through the first ten days. Nonetheless, I resolved there and then that I would not allow this to be one of those occasions where I walked away questioning myself about how I handled something. The whole game had just changed; if I mishandled this one, there was no walking away. I spent the next ten minutes hammering my new doctor with questions: How likely was I to ever see my home again? What are all these medications, and why do I need to take them? Hang on—you just finished telling me I must make it through the next ten days (or else), and now you want me to record everything I eat and drink?? He did not look phased in the slightest, which did not help my feelings of distrust. Why was he not reacting? I realized with a jolt it was because it didn't make any difference: No matter how many questions I asked him, it did not change my situation. It was uncharted territory for me: I was dying, and this man and his team were either going to stop that from happening or they were not.

When he finished his consultation and walked out of the room, I looked at my partner and my dad and asked, "What now?"

My dad quietly replied, "Now we take things one day at a time."

That night, I lay in my hospital bed. Marvin was curled up on the smallest pull-out chair you have ever seen, snoring lightly beside me. I found it impossible to fall asleep, though, knowing there was a genuine possibility I would never wake up. My nighttime nurse offered to give me pills to help me sleep, but I refused. Judging by the new addition to my IV pole—antibiotics to resolve an infection somewhere inside of me—my body was losing the ability to regulate itself. It was tired, but I did not want to take drugs that would make it feel okay to give up.

Instead, I unlocked my phone, opened my text messaging app and started sending messages to people who had inspired me or positively impacted my life. For example, my nail technician, Tuyen (whom I knew as Tracy), is one of the kindest humans I have ever met. She is gentle and funny and always sees the good in people. I aspired to be more like her, and if I was going to die in this bed, I needed her to know that she is one of an army who makes the world worth living in. I scoured social media for friends I had not spoken to in years who had been there for me at some of the lowest points in my life. I wanted them to know that if they never heard from me again, it was not because I did not love them. It was simply because I was not here.

CHAPTER FIVE

THE RIGHT TYPE OF CONTROL

While seeking online information about acute promyelocytic leukemia, I noticed a couple of things rather quickly. First of all, there was a lot of information out there about breast cancer. There were tons of online resources and tons of blogs. I also noticed that many of the online resources I found started with something like, "Make sure you research your options and make the right decision for you."

As I scrolled through the dozens of websites, I thought to myself, "*It would have been nice to have more time to decide. It is unfair that my only option was Princess Margaret Cancer Centre or Juravinski Cancer Centre.*" I suppose opting to do nothing was an option too, but no matter how you slice it, nothing was fair about my situation, and none of the options were great. Period. It meant I would be displaced from my family, in the dead of winter, an hour and a half from home. And worse, none of the resources I found online resonated with me.

Without information to help me understand what was happening to my body, I shot questions at my nurses and doctors like a fully automatic assault rifle as often as I could. What had caused this? Is it genetic? Could my diet have contributed? Not enough sleep? Stress?

In the short time I had already spent in the hospital, I had played out every possible scenario in my head. I needed answers, and I could not find them on my own. At least seven hundred and seventy-six of the one thousand scenarios flitting through my mind included me not making it home after thirty-six days, which was unacceptable. Stewing in this pot of toxicity was not helping. I needed to get a grip. Luckily, I was pretty good at that already: I had often found myself at a crossroads where I'd had to make a conscious decision. Crumble and let life's inevitable hardships overcome me, or put one foot in front of the other and make a move.

Very early in my life, I had found myself in precarious positions, and in the early days, my automatic response was to freeze, but freezing had proven dangerous time and again. So, as hard as it may have been, I learned that putting one foot in front of the other was the only way forward. The problem was that I was not making decisions because they were the right ones to make, rather it was often because of my desire *not* to become some dismal version of myself. While I had managed to accomplish the things I focused on, my successes were driven by the determination to overcome the negativity and difficulty I had faced early in life—backward-facing, rather than forward-facing, if you will.

I recall visiting a friends house as a preteen. We were playing hide and seek, and I had hidden in a spot close to the backyard where several adults sat talking together. I recall overhearing the adults talk about where they thought I would end up in life. They predicted I would be a high school dropout or a drug addict. I could also recall friends sharing with me that their parents had discouraged them from spending time with me. I knew I could be a little bossy and headstrong, but what had I done to make them believe I would be a teenage pregnancy statistic or that I would take their daughters down with me? I never knew. I still don't.

I do know that while many people make decisions that lead to severe outcomes, some come out on the other side of those things perfectly fine. Sure, they have some scars, but they are also stronger, smarter and more experienced. They should not be condemned for making mistakes because, quite frankly, *everyone* makes mistakes.

As a strong-willed young girl, hearing adults making this kind of pronouncement about me was absolutely devastating. Over the ensuing years it caused me great shame and self-doubt. I vowed never to be that person they imagined me to be. Instead—spurred, ironically, by that strong will, I resolved that I would show them exactly who I could be, and that fuelled me until the day I landed in the hospital. It became so ingrained in who I was that, for many years, I lived a life that was not meant for me. So, even though at times I wanted to throw up my hands, stop fighting, stop driving myself forward, to just give up, I could not. It was one step too close to letting them win, and that was inconceivable.

So finding myself here in the hospital bed I told myself to do what had become second nature to me: I told myself to pull up my big-girl pants. Given how hard it had been to find someone who would take me seriously, I felt that I was on my own. So I decided I would focus on what I could control. Mentally at least, I put one foot in front of the other, determined to walk myself right out of this mess. I began by creating a list of things I wanted to do when I was clear of this unfortunate life event. To begin with, I wanted to build an online resource so that the next time someone diagnosed with acute leukemia searched for help, they would find my lessons learned and all the resources I had found.

But first, I needed to make it out of that hospital alive. No matter what I had done leading up to this moment or how I had contributed to this unpleasant life pause, I could not change where I was. So, I stopped focusing on the things that were uncontrollable. Every minute and every ounce of energy counted, and focusing on things out of my control was hazardous. Instead, I set my sights on two things:

1. What can I do right now to help myself and my medical team?
2. What future goals are so non-negotiable that I must live to experience them?

The first was relatively simple under the circumstances. My body needed three things to have a fighting chance of making it out of the hospital alive: nutrition, rest, and movement. There were some rules about what I could or could not eat during the early days. Since the chemotherapy was wiping out both the good and bad cells, making me neutropenic—meaning it was impossible for my immune system to function—it was important to avoid foods that might contain bacteria that our bodies can otherwise tolerate. I also began searching for information to learn which foods would help my immune system recover and started eating more of those foods.

Rest was easy. I got lots of that.

Movement was a bit more of a challenge, since I was cooped up in the hospital and tethered to an IV. But then I got creative. Every day a pleasant young woman visited my room to change the sheets on my bed. Even on the worst days, I felt awkward about someone caring for my bed, so I began politely declining and changing my own sheets every day. Was it necessary? No, but it was an opportunity to move my body, and doing so would help my lymphatic system eliminate the strong cytotoxic chemicals cycling through my body meant to destroy my cancerous cells.

Did I truly have any control over whether I would make it out of that hospital? Some say not, but for my own sanity I needed to focus on things that would give me the best shot of getting out of there. Even though occasionally we all must admit defeat, wallowing in that defeat—or dwelling on the possibility of it—does not promote healing.

The second point, my future goals, was far more than a bucket list. Some things were non-negotiable in my life. I simply could not cease to exist because there were things I *needed* to live for. I *needed* to get married. I *needed* to take my kids on a Disney cruise. I *needed* to watch them graduate from university. These things were my unconditional needs. They became my mantra, the shining star that guided me out of the swirling pit of darkness and back to clarity. In hindsight, the nights leading up to that moment had been terrifying. So much so that I would not let the nurses medicate me for fear I would never wake up. But now that I had snapped out of it, there was work to do. I needed all the energy I could muster. So at last, decision made, I asked for the sleeping pills that night and took my rest.

CHAPTER SIX

(ALMOST) NO REGRETS

2013

It was just weeks after my return to work from maternity leave. Going back to work after a year of settling into motherhood was an adjustment. My priorities had shifted, and things that previously seemed like a big deal became trivial. While I could not put my finger on it at the time, there was a sort of self-assuredness that I had gained through the experience of motherhood that I had not previously possessed. One thing that had not changed, and was very much amplified, was how I felt about my body. I had spent the last year trying to learn to love my post-pregnancy body, and most days, it was still a struggle. When I returned to my job, most of my work clothes no longer fit, and I looked a little different than I had previously. I felt shame and embarrassment. One particular day, I sat at my desk eating lunch when a well-respected male colleague walked by, stopped in my doorway and asked, "Hey, does your belly look like Homer Simpson's face after being pregnant?"

Something inside me quietly snapped. I had spent years conforming to toxic work culture. I had endured heinous behaviour, had shrunk myself and quieted my morals to have a seat at the table. Yet, every time I found myself in these kinds of interactions with others, it felt like they walked away with a piece of me. I knew I did not deserve that type of treatment, yet I always let it happen. I questioned myself about why I allowed such behaviour. Often, as women, even when we are defending ourselves we are viewed unfavorably. But I feared it was also because I personally gained from being there, and so I chose not to rock the boat. Even after several years of enduring such behaviour, I could not shield myself from the onslaught of self-deprecating thoughts and feelings his comment invoked.

After years of dealing with these types of personal attacks, I suddenly felt that I could no longer sit by and accept them. I'm not sure if that particular interaction was the final straw simply because of how vile his question had been or whether it was a culmination of both the personal attacks and my own guilt over never having spoken up for myself. Memories rolled through my consciousness like a film reel, reminding me of how often I had sat at that table, quietly preserving my seat there, fully aware of the discrimination that was taking place and how it would impact other people who deserved to be sitting there too. Enough was enough. I was done conforming, shrinking myself—and, ultimately, contributing to the problem. I would no longer take it, and that moment became the catalyst for change.

On the way home from the gym, I called a friend to recount the day's event. I was angry as hell, but I also felt hurt, frustrated, and ashamed because the truth was that my body no longer looked the same and it bothered me. My colleague's remark had hit a nerve—just as he'd intended it to—and as the mom of a one-year-old, I already grappled with the stigma of being a single mother.

My friend listened sympathetically and then said, "Why do you care what they say?"

I reflected and then replied, "I don't know."

She said, "They don't live your life. They do not feel what you feel. At the end of the day, your life does not impact them. So why live your life to meet their expectations? Just live your life for yourself and your daughter. You are the only one who needs to be okay with it."

It was like a light bulb lit up in my head. It seemed so obvious, yet until that moment, I did not realize that I had, in fact, been endlessly, pointlessly, trying to meet the expectations of others. I had spent an exorbitant amount of time ruminating, replaying scenarios just like the one I had found myself in earlier that day, thinking about how I could have handled them better. The witty things I could have said, how I could have hidden my reaction better, how I could have shot back and made them feel what I felt. I could not even be sure who I was more upset with—them, or myself for not responding differently.

Suddenly, I realized that how I responded to them, or not, was never the issue. What was more important was the reason I cared so much about what anyone else thought. At the end of the day, those adults who had said those terrible things about me as a child —and who accidentally motivated me to strive for greatness—had not been part of my life for nearly two decades, yet their awful words still resonated in my mind. I lived with it daily whereas they had likely forgotten who I was. And, similarly, even though I worked daily with this so-called professional who had regularly verbally abused me (and others) for years, he would likely forget me one day, too. At one time, the thought of being forgotten would have been terrifying, but as I developed confidence, I realized that I did not want everyone to remember me. I did not *need* everyone to remember me, especially not people who intently chose to mistreat me.

It was time to unsubscribe from the constructs that any person, team or organization expected me to exist within. I had worked myself nearly to death to be relevant, to prove my value, and to try to keep up with what I perceived as the successes of my friends, family and colleagues. I decided I would not take any new regrets or shame into my possession. They serve no purpose.

Sure, how we react to others is an essential component of human communication and connection. How we respond to others teaches them how we want to be or do not want to be treated. But more importantly, how we react to others is dependent on the relationship we have with ourselves. If we have a loving relationship with ourselves first, if we are confident in ourselves and self-affirming, then the personal attacks of others often won't land. The opinions and expectations of others become irrelevant. That is not to say that we entirely disregard others. Rather, we hold sacred the bonds we have with those who are deserving of our love and attention. However, when our boundaries are at risk, those boundaries —and ourselves—come first.

To return to that pivotal day in the office, I had to ask myself, what about me made that person believe he could ask such a despicable question? And why did I regret not snapping back with something just as callous? I knew I could reflect on such experiences in a self-punishing way, but instead, I chose to reflect with self-compassion on why I allowed it to impact me in the first place.

Regrets are always related to something from the past, and until the day comes that we finally build a time machine, there is nothing we can do to change the circumstances that lead to the discomfort we all feel when we experience it. But what if we change the way we *look* at regret?

I realized that the validation and acceptance I sought in the workplace were not limited to that space. I had always strived for the approval of the people around me. I was sailing through life in the dark, and they were the lighthouses I thought would stop me from crashing into the shore. I had lacked the boundaries and self-worth to look inward which always meant that even when others were well-intentioned, I may have been operating beyond my ability to do so. *I* was the only lighthouse I had ever needed. I just didn't know it yet.

It was time for me to start trusting myself, listening to myself, and loving myself. Sure, it was going to be a bumpy ride for a while. After all, no one is an expert when they start something new. It would require grace and self-forgiveness—and I was going to start down the road to those things by building my first guardrail. I promised myself that for the rest of my days, anytime I was uncertain about something, I would decide how to proceed based on the answer to one crucial question: *Will I be able to lay my head down at night, okay with the choice I make?*

If the answer was yes, then I could live with the potential outcome of my decision, good or bad. If the answer was no, that I could not live with the possible consequences that choice might bring, then I knew I'd need to make a different choice. And if the answer was yes and there were still undesirable consequences, it would not then be fair for me to beat myself up about it because I would know that I had made the best decision I could with the information I had available.

Sometimes things do not go the way we plan. Sometimes, we have no control over certain variables, and all too often we perceive those scenarios as our fault. *I should have known better.* It makes trusting ourselves feel risky, but if we cannot trust ourselves, we surely cannot determine who else can be trusted.

Feeling guilt over things we do or decisions we make is inevitable. At times, it is even useful. If we have well-established morals, ethics and integrity, guilt can act as our compass and create accountability. It is an opportunity to learn and to do better next time. But if we do not have well-established morals, ethics and integrity, that same feeling of guilt may translate as shame. Shame is like a loudspeaker in our minds telling us over and over that we are not worthy. It is detrimental and will spiral us into self-loathing, which serves no one and certainly not ourselves.

Up until that time, I had spent too much time feeling shameful. I had made decisions based on what society taught me I should do, and when it did not feel right, I pushed that feeling down and asked myself what was wrong with *me*. Throughout the entire second decade of my life, I told myself I should be more like my mom or like the moms of friends. They were always taking care of the people around them. Even TV commercials modelled mothers who sacrificed everything for their family, so who did I think I was to choose to have fun, or to pursue a hobby, or, worse, to do nothing at all—to rest? Though I sometimes decided to do what I truly wanted, I would then beat myself up for not working hard enough, for being selfish, and would tell myself that something was wrong with me. But what was wrong was I was not being true to myself. I was not allowing myself to grow into the person I should have been. Instead, I was stifling her. Telling her she was broken.

I reflected on being shamed at work for the changes to my body after giving birth, and I thought about how my body had done a magical thing. It had grown a whole new human, and while my body had changed, it had done so to bring a vibrant life into the world. A human who, no doubt, is going to make a meaningful mark. And that was something to be proud of.

I reflected on that mean-spirited colleague standing over my shoulder and found myself chuckling at his ignorance, and I decided that his insidious question would not hurt me—*he* would no longer hurt me. He would not have the privilege of watching me wince or hide in shame because his validation was no longer the marker of my progress, worth or validity in this world. In fact, when I stopped spending so much time beating myself up, I realized that the perpetrator was a far cry from the perfectionism that he, too, seemed desperate to achieve. Somewhat to my surprise, rather than capitalizing on his pain, I found myself feeling sorry for him.

The journey to self-love is not linear. I was cautiously optimistic that I had taken a step in the right direction, but that is just what it was—one step of hundreds, maybe thousands, that I would need to continue choosing to take. I still looked back with shame at my teenage, naïve self who had made some bad decisions, but I did so less and less frequently as time went on. I had successfully set my first boundary and committed to sticking with it. I had learned to take responsibility for my decisions, and to be forgiving of myself when they turned out to be the wrong ones because I am human, after all. Sometimes it felt impossible, but I was beginning to learn that unlearning and relearning takes time, and building new habits is never a straight path to consistency. Sometimes getting to consistency is that much more challenging when the people around us are comfortable with us as we are, and specifically with how malleable we are. We must be especially vigilant of people who discredit or doubt the direction we choose to move in, because these are the very people who stand to benefit from our lack of boundaries.

The process of unlearning and relearning can be likened to walking out from the center of a spiral (See Fig 1). At the beginning, the twists and turns are tight, and we are likely to revert to old habits more often—to trip and fall—but as long as we get back up, dust ourselves off, and keep going, the twists and turns of the spiral lengthen. It may feel disorienting, even scary, but change typically is. If we stick with it, the frequency of reverting also lessens. As long as we take responsibility for our own choices and actions and do our best, there is no room for regret and shame, and there is certainly no room for the negativity or abuse of others. There is only room for new lessons and progress.

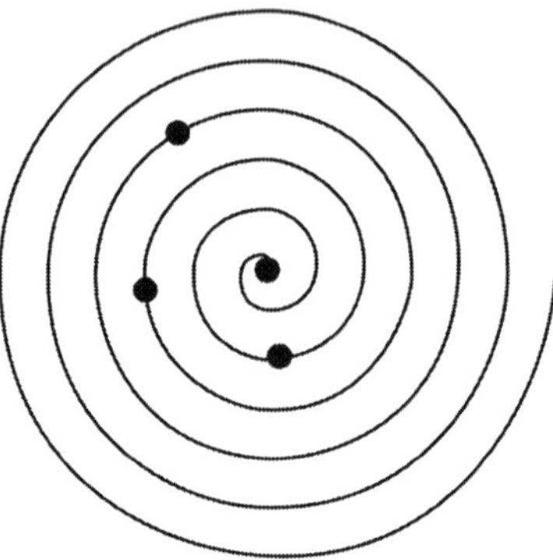

Figure 1

CHAPTER SEVEN

PERSPECTIVE

Marvin and I started dating in August 2015. Our relationship has always been unique. He is very ambitious, stoic, independent, and responsible. He is confident and has always accepted me for who I am. I am determined, passionate, maybe a little dramatic and free-spirited. Together we have always managed life well. The bills are paid on time, there are always groceries in the fridge, even if I myself have not visited the grocery store, and our kids eat way more vegetables than I ever did growing up. As a blended family, we also have free and childless time that most other parents are not so lucky to have. Pre-pandemic, we enjoyed fine dining, dancing, barhopping or movie nights as though we were still newly dating. Occasionally, we spent time independently with friends. Always without jealously, suspicion or possessive responses. On paper, we were perfect.

Marvin and I were together for one year before we experienced our first trauma together. It was a sudden loss neither of us expected and was our first lesson in how we would manage life's speed bumps as partners. I was torn up, sad, and mad, and my coping strategy had always been to hide behind anger and independence. He was torn up, sad, and mad, and his coping strategy was to withdraw. It was the start of a very lonely time in our relationship. Over the course of the next year and a half, we experienced two more traumas, again, unexpected life events that were like being hit by a freight train, spun around on the tracks—and being smoked by the train coming the other way, too.

Somewhere between these events, maybe after the third, we realized that something was not working for us. We were together and still getting things done, but we were both lonely and resentful. Over a series of heated arguments, we concluded that we needed to start talking to each other—and not just the typical "What would you like for dinner?" or "How was your day, honey?" kind of talk. Rather, we had to start talking about our needs and our life plans, and we needed to have compassion for each other. It was the beginning of a significant shift in our relationship. We had a long way to go, but we started to see what we needed for ourselves and from each other.

I can remember Marvin and I having an exchange in August 2017 that went something like this:

Him: "I want to marry you."

Me: "We have issues we need to work out before we agree to commit the rest of our lives together, and I'm not sure we can work them out."

Marvin was anxious to pop the question, and I, being a perfectionist, had made it clear that I might not be able to say yes if he proposed. As I'm sure you can imagine, this could, in fact, have been the end of our relationship.

I was a thirty-six-year-old woman with a five-year-old daughter, and I had never been married. Though there were times I faced judgment for having a child out of wedlock, as they used to call it, I felt that getting pregnant had never been a good enough reason for me to marry. Marriage was supposed to be sacred. About love, respect and mutual admiration. Marvin and I had already been to hell and back, or at least what we perceived as hell then, and had just started figuring out what we needed from each other. It just did not seem like the right time. I needed to be entirely sure that the challenges we faced in our relationship were resolved before we took that leap. So, for the time being, marriage was off the table.

I was fourteen years old when my parents separated. Almost thirty years later, I still remember vividly what it was like witnessing and being a part of that. I remember the irrational emotions and words that sliced to the bone. The sadness and insecurity it caused my brother and me as children. If I were ever to marry, it would have to be the right person and the right circumstances, because I never wanted to go through that feeling again, and I certainly did not want to put my children through it.

Four months after Marvin declared his desire to marry, I found myself sitting in a room of the local emergency department waiting to find out which cancer center could accept me to begin treatment. As soon as the doctor revealed my bloodwork results, I placed a frantic call to Marvin and asked him to meet me at the hospital. Even though at the time of the call, he was at work forty kilometers away, he was by my side within an hour. As soon as he walked through the hospital room door, I could see the worry etched in his face. I could see how much I meant to him. He sat on the chair beside the bed while we waited for the doctor to make the arrangements for me at the cancer centre. Quietly I said, "I realize we have been through a lot already. If you want to walk away right now, I will harbor no hard feelings and wish you well."

Those were some of the hardest words I've ever spoken, but I meant every one: we had already been through so much and we were just beginning to pick up the pieces. After all, we were only in our mid-thirties, and there was so much more life to live. He did not need to stick around to deal with a sick girlfriend who might not even live through the next few months. But with no hesitation whatsoever, he declined my offer. He stayed.

On the day that I arrived at Juravinski Cancer Centre, the commotion calmed, and it was just Marvin and me. Once I was settled in my room, he got into bed with me, and we cuddled. I remember distinctly lying there in his arms and feeling comforted by his presence. I was grateful he had decided to stay. My mind drifted back to his question from four months before. I thought about what I had perceived as so significant that we must pause the progression of our relationship. What had seemed like such hurdles to me that we needed to overcome them before I would agree to marry him? Even a few hours ago, before the day had exploded into medical chaos, it had still seemed like our relationship was hanging in the balance on some miracle fix that would set everything "right" so we could move on. But lying there in the bed, feeling his warmth, I could no longer make sense of what had seemed so earth-shattering. All the things that had made such sense and seemed so logical, so terribly important, just hours ago suddenly ... evaporated.

Over the years, I had watched many spousal relationships develop among my family and friends. At times, one of them would come to me, angry and upset, and confide in me about whatever thing their partner had said or done. Often, my advice in the face of these difficulties was the same: *Get out!* It was part of a pattern for me, I realized: I myself had often wanted to run, to leave bad situations, but had been unable to find the strength to leave even when the alarm bells sounded in my mind. But the people who came to me still had the chance to get out before it was too late!

And as I sit here and write, I now see the irony in my telling Marvin to run when the doctor delivered the bad news. That, too, was part of the pattern.

Most of the time, though, the people I advised to run did no such thing; they unburdened themselves to me and then went back to their loved ones. I found this perplexing. Why did they accept being treated in ways that hurt them? The epiphany hit me like a ton of bricks, and my perspective shifted. All the things they loved about their partners made the crappy times worth it. And more importantly, they had faith that they would get through it together. It was most certainly not because their relationships were magically perfect. Rather, they accepted their partners, warts and all, and agreed to work together through the good and the bad.

That is what Marvin had done. He had chosen to accept our relationship and all that came with it. He chose to have faith that we would work through it together no matter what life threw at us. Would all those unresolved issues have made a difference in the grand scheme of things if I was going to die in that hospital bed anyway? The answer was no. It would not have made a difference because as I lay there in that bed, not knowing if I would live to experience any of those resolutions I so staunchly expected, I realized all that mattered was that he was there.

And what's more, if we had decided to split when those unforeseen challenges arose or if Marvin had chosen to walk when I opened that door and invited him to do so, would it have been worth the loss? Before I got sick, my pride would have said, "Yes, I warned him ...." I would have buried the deep pain and told myself he did not deserve me. But the fact is, it would have been a lie and a devastating tragedy. It seemed like such a simple concept, but I could not see it until we were in the shitstorm of our latest trauma.

I had rarely ended a relationship feeling that the person I was leaving was a kind human that I simply did not connect with intimately. Almost without fail, breakups felt dramatic, intense and unhappy. But as I assessed the state of my relationship with Marvin, the early days of dealing with our shared trauma revisited me. I had always believed that responding with anger and independence was self-protecting. For many years, it was automatic: If I put a barrier between us, it would somehow hurt less. But the reality was, it did not hurt less. In fact, it was what created the chasm between me and others, perpetuating the loneliness and resentment.

Enduring this shared trauma was different; there was no one to direct my anger at, no way for me to exercise my independence anymore, as my literal survival depended on healthcare professionals. The only thing I could do was cling to the familiarity of my partner. It was undoubtedly the most vulnerable feeling in the world. But in that vulnerability, I observed something new: rather than pulling away and withdrawing, Marvin responded. He held me a little tighter. Rather than hide in the washroom as the feelings forced their way out, he cried with me.

There is no doubt that at one time, my angry and fierce displays of independence were useful, necessary even. Those tactics had been helpful when my anxious attachment style told me I must make every relationship work. They had helped protect me in relationships where safety was not guaranteed. But in a healthy relationship, when two people genuinely care for each other, that need dissipates. And the result of using unhealthy tactics in a genuinely loving relationship is a lot of cycling hurt.

Life was never going to be perfect. We were never going to be without challenges, so waiting to marry until everything was perfect meant I would be robbing myself, him and our children of an opportunity, holding us both to an impossible standard. It came down to whether we were equally willing to put in the effort to work on the existing challenges and all the other difficulties that would arise through the course of our lives. It became crystal clear to me that marriage, commitment, and love are not about perfection. They are about trusting your partner to uphold the sacredness of vulnerability, and, despite our anger and despite our desire to lash out, to choose compassion instead. They are about picking each other over and over again when things get tough, and remembering that as long as the fundamental basics of a relationship exist —respect, consideration, loyalty—it's okay to show our hurt. The bottom line is that in the difficult times, we choose to steer the bow into the waves to ride them out together, holding the good times close to us as we try to understand each other better.

And this, I realized, is why those who had confided in me had not taken my advice, had not run.

"I'm ready now," I said as we lay together.

He responded, "Ready for what?"

I said, "I'm ready to get married."

"Are you proposing to me?" he said cheekily.

"No. I'm proposing you propose to *me*!"

And for a few moments, we lay there, holding each other tight, and laughed freely, forgetting the gravity of our situation.

As Christmas approached, many of the regular nurses on the ward were off spending well-deserved time with their families. The hallways were quieter, the nurses on duty less familiar. My oncologist had taken time off to be with his family too. The doctor filling in for him came into my room for a regular check-up a few days before Christmas. He checked my chart and asked questions, and when he determined my body was stable enough, he offered an overnight "pass" to go home for Christmas. Terror crashed through my body like a wrecking ball. I thanked him for the offer and explained that I had been told I would have to be there for thirty-six days, and I wanted to do everything I could to give myself the best shot at survival, so I would stay. Each time a new nurse visited me, they would ask if I was going home for Christmas, and I would tell them I was staying put. They all said, "Oh, that's too bad." But I would reassure them it was fine. No doubt it would be the most memorable Christmas I had ever had!

I had finished the four-dose course of Idarubicin, a chemotherapy ominously nicknamed "The Red Devil," and narrowly made it through without any major setbacks. Yes, the mucositis had shut me up for days, my heart rate had dropped to thirty eight beats per minute requiring me to walk around with a heart monitor for more than a week, and we had finally entered negotiations around what I would need to do to avoid a feeding tube. The pain in my back and bones equalled the pain of child labour, but I had made it through the first milestone without an aneurism, heart failure or flatlining, so there was much to celebrate.

By the time the holidays arrived, eating was nearly impossible, and my ability to continue morning walks on the ward had diminished. I had begun losing weight, no longer trusted my legs, and my hair was falling out. Despite the exhaustion and pain, I had stayed more active than you would imagine a cancer patient to be. But I had grown weary. I was glad I had opted to stay in the hospital for Christmas. I felt like my ability to maintain any amount of independence was slipping away.

But to my delight, since I had opted to remain in the hospital for Christmas, my family decided to bring Christmas to me! Of course, it was not the Christmas Eve we had counted on—we had planned to host thirty of our closest family members and friends at our home that evening. We had bought fancy new dresses for our daughters, who were so excited to show them off. However, we were determined to make the best of it. My family arrived at the hospital around dinnertime on Christmas Eve. Our kids arrived with their dads. Victoria's dad was accompanied by his parents. The girls wore their beautiful new dresses, and my dad and stepmom even brought a trolley with all our presents in tow. My mom brought a big blanket, and we all headed to the Outpatient Day Service (ODS) waiting room. ODS was closed for the evening, so we had it all to ourselves. Everyone piled in and picked a spot. There was no shortage of seating.

My mom spread the blanket the floor, where my daughters sat anxiously awaiting their presents, and we had Christmas. The only thing missing was the turkey. It certainly wasn't how any of us expected to spend Christmas together, but it was special in its own right, and I will never forget it. The pure, unguarded love of everyone in the room was palpable. Victoria's grandmother had helped her pick out a gift for me. When I opened the box, inside lay a scarf and some matching jewellery. The scarf was silky and brilliantly colored. I burst into tears and hugged Victoria.

Previously, it had not been so evident that I was ill, but I knew that at this point, the people who surrounded me could see the impact of the disease and the treatment. There was a gentleness among them that I had not previously observed. It was beautiful.

Around that time, many people had said to me, "It must suck to be stuck there for the holidays! Can't you get a day pass?" I had responded, "I am alive. I am grateful. And I get to spend another Christmas with my family, even if it's in the hospital." That was all that mattered.

Marvin had gone home early the next morning to be with Isabelle for a few hours. He returned later that day while my dad and stepmom were visiting. We fondly reflected on the previous evening's event and talked and laughed. Marvin, a man of very few words, even cracked a couple of jokes. As I sat in my comfy chair by the window, Marvin stood before me with his laptop in hand and offered it to me. I was confused. He insisted I take it, so I did.

I opened the screen to a PowerPoint slideshow featuring photos of our daughters. The pictures must have been taken the evening before. They were wearing their fancy Christmas dresses and were standing in front of the gigantic, regal tree in the hospital's foyer, smiling and laughing together. I began to flip through the slides. In each one, each of them held a piece of paper with a note written on it. Their messages told the story that my girls loved me, and that Marvin did too. In the final shot, the girls held up a note asking me if I would marry him. I shifted my gaze to Marvin, who stood in front of me and took his sweater off. He wore a white t-shirt with "#Marry Me" painted in red and green to represent the season. I stood up and hugged him before he even had a chance to get down on one knee. He placed the engagement ring on my finger, and there we stood, embracing in my hospital room in the presence of our family. I had my chemotherapy hung on my IV pole, and I was swollen from all the medication pumping into my body. It was Christmas Day, and I was still not convinced I would even live to see the wedding. But despite all that, we were engaged.

What many assumed would be a depressing holiday season became the most heartfelt and memorable one of our lives. Had I held onto the trivial issues that seemed so monumental at one time, who knows what would have happened?

I was proud of us and looked optimistically forward to our future together. While I could not quite articulate what I felt then, I know now that it was certainty amid the uncertain. Who knew what life was going to throw at us next? But whatever it was, we would always be there to support each other through it.

CHAPTER EIGHT
LOSING MY ARMOR

Prior to meeting Marvin, the love of my life, my first boyfriend from high school and I reconnected. There was something soothing about the company of someone who had known me at such an innocent time in life, before adulthood's mistakes and hardships inevitably changed us. He lived on the west coast and I just outside of Toronto, but through the power of the internet, we were able to talk, chat and see each other often.

One evening we reminisced about when we knew each other as very young people.

"I remember those days well. We were so innocent then," I told him.

"I don't know about that," he said with a chuckle.

"I mean, we did not know much about the world then. It had not changed us yet. We are different now." I was quiet for a moment, allowing myself to grieve the loss of who I had been.

"But I know you," he said. "You are not this person you project to the world. I think you feel like you need to have a tough shell, and I get why. But it is not who you are."

"That is nice of you, but time and experience change people," I protested. "I am not that person you knew all those years ago."

I think that version of me he remembered was who he wanted me to be. I knew he cared deeply for that version of me. She was naïve, too trusting, and vulnerable. She had been soft, and she got hurt a lot.

Those days were long gone. This version of me was tough, determined and in control. The cruel world had made sure of that.

I DISCOVERED THE MARY KAY WEBSITE WHEN I WAS IN my mid-twenties. It was one of the first simulation websites I ever visited. I remember being so excited that I could load a picture of myself on the website and then try out different makeup and hairstyles. For its time, it was state of the art. I tried out different makeup looks, with varying degrees of success. The wedding looks were both terrible and hilarious. If I had planned on walking down the aisle looking like I had been on an all-night bender, those were the looks I would have gone for. I also tried different hairstyles and hair colors. My hair had always been very long. I tried curly looks, layered looks, highlights and lowlights. I simply could not get enough of that tool! When I had exhausted all long-to-medium-length hairstyles, even the most ridiculous ones, I got curious about the short ones. I clicked through them, rejecting even the possibility of doing such a thing to my hair—until I landed on a platinum-blonde pixie cut. I was intrigued. I stared at the image of myself with super short, bright blonde hair, assessing how I felt about it. It made me feel something, but I was not quite sure what it was. Did I like it? A pixie?! Platinum?!

There was no denying it. "OMG, YES!" I fell in love. I ran to my bedroom, knelt beside my bed and pulled out the large storage bin that held proof of my life experiences and the digital camera that had captured at least some of them. I sat back down in front of my computer screen and snapped a photo. In those days, it was not as easy as taking a screenshot with a cellphone. Sending a text to say "Hello" took thirteen clicks on the keypad, and screens were still on a grayscale. So, I carried my camera with me everywhere in the coming days to debate my love affair with this cut and color with friends.

Some loved it. Some thought it was extreme. Some outright shut it down. No matter, I could not get that hairstyle out of my head.

Ten years later, I found myself standing at a work colleague's desk talking about hairstyles; she herself had a very short cut, and her natural hair color was so blonde it was almost white. She wanted to cut her hair shorter but was unsure. I said, "You should totally do it! You only live once, right?"

She said, "You're right. I just don't know."

"I wish I had the guts to do it," I confessed. "Ten years ago, I found this hairstyle, much like the one you mentioned, that I fell in love with but I could never pull the trigger."

"You could totally pull it off! You should do it. If you hate it, it's just hair. It will grow back," she said enthusiastically.

Tempting as it was, I still could not do it after all those years.

On some level, I always knew why. I would never have uttered the words out loud, but I knew. I had spent my entire life being told I should be a certain way, either directly or through reinforcing behaviours. Look a certain way, speak (or not) a certain way so people would like me. For me, as I aged, that meant I was always chasing unattainable goals. The size on the tag of my jeans was never small enough. I laughed too loud, my jokes were inappropriate, and I was never pretty enough. As a young adult, I went on starvation diets at least twice a year and could not tolerate the quiet because my self-talk would not stop scolding me for every mistake I had made. And no matter what, *never* cut your hair because short hair is for boys. My life experiences had told me that it was not desirable for a woman to have a mind of her own. It was most desirable for a woman to "take care of" others and she should always do her best to be attractive. No matter how much I loved that platinum pixie, I feared cutting my hair off. I knew it would look fantastic, but I couldn't shake the thought that it would make me stand out in a crowd. My womanhood would be questioned, and my desirability as a young(ish) woman diminished. The idea made me feel insecure.

But all those years later, I still thought about that hairstyle frequently.

On Christmas Day, only an hour after proposing marriage, Marvin and I went into my hospital bathroom to cut my hair. I wanted desperately for the strands to stop falling out. I prayed that my pillow would not be covered in hair when I woke up, but it was futile. I asked my nurses about it. They said some people use the cold-capping method, which is basically a cap that some people wear on their heads with ice packs in them, to avoid losing hair in the first place, but given the nature of my illness, we were already well beyond that point. They said that others decided to just buzz their heads to get it over with. They mentioned that some women felt that by doing so empowered them because they were taking "control" of the situation rather than watching the chemo ravage their femininity. I knew I was not ready to accept that eventuality. So, with me sitting on a chair in the bathroom and Marvin standing behind me with the scissors, he got to work.

He started by making a ponytail and cutting off everything below the elastic band holding what was left of my beautiful long blonde locks. I must admit that, sitting in that chair, I learned that my fiancé, an aircraft maintenance engineer, would also have made a great hairstylist! He cut my hair into an inverted bob with an undercut and, under such grim circumstances, even made the experience fun by pretending to be a mad scientist making his creation come to life! I anticipated it would be devastating. I thought for sure I would cry. Instead, we laughed and made the best of it together.

As the days went by, I got used to my new look. I missed my long hair, but the cute short bob was not so bad. Despite all that was happening, I still did not think I looked like a sick person. I am unsure whether that was because I desperately clung to life and insisted on seeing a healthy person in the mirror; it's a good possibility. I could still tell myself that we had cut my hair short because it was what I wanted to do rather than what I *needed* to do. As the days went by, my remaining hair became brittle and matted. It covered everything: my pillow, blankets, bedsheets, clothes, and the floor of my room. When the cleaning lady visited every afternoon, I apologized for the mess, though she was probably used to it, and frankly, I couldn't have stopped it from falling out if I tried. But I apologized nonetheless.

My scalp hurt so bad. It felt like a headache on the outside of my head. I began wearing headwraps to manage the hair fall—and my emotions—as the patchiness of my scalp started to show through. As the days went by, I did begin to look sick, and I could no longer keep up the illusion that I was fine. The dread crept in. I felt frantic and panicked, and my belly always hurt.

One morning, when the nurse shifts changed and my nurse of the day came into my room, she announced that I was being discharged later that day. I could not hold back my gut reaction to the news. I had expected I would be in the hospital for thirty-six days, and it was only day twenty-one. How could they be sending me home fifteen days early?

One might think that kind of news would inspire celebration. Truth be told, I would have thought the same thing had I not been the one experiencing it. Though I had barely spoken at all in the preceding days due to the constant, exploding pain in my mouth, my response was instantaneous and firm.

"No."

She looked at me, a little shocked and perplexed. But I stood firm. I was in no way, shape or form ready to leave the safety of the hospital. Granted, I did not sleep well most nights because of vitals checks and the multiple IV lines that still ran twenty-three hours daily. Once my liver had started functioning better on its own, I was allowed total freedom from my tubes for a shower and a walk around the ward, if I had enough energy, for one hour a day. But even in the midst of that "freedom," I was under constant observation. I felt reassured, knowing that if anything went sideways, even in that hour, the nurses would arrive in a flash. There would be no regular bloodwork happening at six-hour intervals at home. No nurses checking to make sure I was still breathing at night. No one trained to administer CPR if my heart finally gave up. Practically every moment of my life was monitored and planned for me now. Thankfully, I was able to negotiate one more day in the hospital to help mentally prepare for my discharge. I suppose the upside was that, for a moment, it distracted me from the sadness of losing my hair, and I was living for the small wins.

I CRIED THE WHOLE WAY HOME THE NEXT DAY. I AM pretty sure Marvin was confused. It should have been a happy milestone. It *was* happy, but it was a lot of other things too. I've never quite understood why we view emotional ambivalence—the simultaneous experience of both positive and negative emotions, or a feeling of being torn—as bad. In my case, I feared leaving my safety net at the hospital and being solely responsible for what medication I needed to take at what time.

The stark reality of the last twenty-two days started to sink in. When I had first been admitted, the odds I would leave the hospital still breathing had been extremely low, but there I was on my way home—what a beautiful thought, to be with my children again. I was so eager to see them. I felt excited to sleep in my own bed, yet afraid of what might happen overnight. The emotions washed over me like wave after wave crashing onto the seashore. All the control, toughness and strength I had built up in the years after last seeing my teenage flame were gone. Maybe he had been right. Perhaps I had been that same soft, emotional girl all along.

TWO DAYS HAD PASSED SINCE I ARRIVED HOME. I WAS still figuring out how to live in my own house as a sick person. Cooking, cleaning, and taking care of the kids were things that I had believed to be my responsibility before becoming ill. But now, everyday tasks had become daunting and, at times, impossible. Hell, I was lucky if I could have a proper shower on my own. It was an adjustment for our five-year-old girls, too, as they no longer had the freedom to treat Mommy like a jungle gym. Between the grogginess of the medications, the pain in my bones, and simply not having energy, I could not play with them the way I used to, and they struggled with that, as did I.

My hair was still falling out everywhere, and there was no cleaner to help with the mess at home. So, on December 31st, New Year's Eve, Marvin plugged his electric razor into a kitchen outlet. I sat on a chair with a towel around my shoulders and another on the floor. I hung my head low and sobbed, listening to the buzzer hum and feeling the odd sensation of the cold metal rub across my scalp. I watched the matted clumps of hair fall to the ground and felt deep sorrow, for it was not just hair that fell; it was my armor. It felt as though the enemy had sliced off the straps, and all at once, I became totally exposed. After a lifetime of relentlessly working to build and maintain the persona of a desirable woman, the one thing that was undeniably desirable, undeniably feminine, and undoubtedly beautiful about me fell. My hair would no longer validate me, hide me from the world, or keep my secrets. On a subconscious level, I had known for many years that it acted as a cloak. It helped me feel invisible, and at times it made me feel protected.

As I stood, Marvin brushed off the last of the fallen strands from my shoulders and I walked to the mirror. My stomach sank. The sorrow deepened. The only part of my experience that was relatable to the movies I had seen about cancer patients was exactly what I saw in the mirror. But I wasn't wearing makeup. It was just me. I felt hideous. Like my very identity had been cut away. Conflict consumed me. I recalled the voices of others saying, "It's just hair," "It will grow back," "But you will look badass bald." I questioned whether I should just be grateful. Perhaps it *was* just hair. But as much as I wanted to believe it, as much as I did not want to appear vain, I could not accept what I saw.

The first few days were the hardest. Between adjusting to the constant feeling of exposure and the menopausal-like symptoms caused by the chemotherapy, I struggled with wearing anything on my head for too long. I was miserable, freezing and then burning up, but the headwraps and hats never left my head.

Then one day, as I sat in the Outpatient Day Services ward waiting for another treatment, my friend Rick walked in. I saw him step in, scan the room and spot me. He set his target and walked straight toward me. He greeted me with the biggest smile and said, "How are you holding up, kid?"

I met Rick on my thirty-seventh birthday, not long after I began treatment. Family and friends had come to visit me in the hospital that evening. We gathered in the patient lounge, and there on the adjacent couch sat the first person I could relate to since being admitted to the hospital. He had been kind and funny, and much as it bugged me at the time, I think back fondly to him always calling me "kid."

I told him I was okay. Another day, another chemo treatment. He pointed at my hat and then said, "I have a surprise for you." Although he had finished most of his treatment months ago, and his hair had grown back, he took his hat off and showed me his bald head. He said, "I know how hard it is, so I shaved my hair off so you wouldn't feel alone." He asked me to take my hat off so we could take a picture together, so, reluctantly, I did.

I did not leave my seat without my hat in those early days, though Rick had gifted me the courage to sit in my assigned spot without it. I felt immense embarrassment but did not want to put it back on, though often I would when I got up. One day I sat in my seat, wanting to get up for water but not wanting to put my hat on. I debated getting up quickly for my water without my hat. Eventually, I did it. I walked intently, eyes on the jug, walking as quickly as I could, praying no one was watching, and then panic came over me. A man, the caregiver of his ill wife, walked up to me and said, "Excuse me, *(no!)* I just want you to know that I'm glad to see you without a hat. I keep telling my wife she should do the same. Maybe if she sees you without yours, she will take hers off too." I thanked him and went back to my seat thinking about what the man had said. I could barely look at myself in the mirror, but this man saw my bold bald head as a positive thing.

As my body recovered from the first round of treatment, I began finding the energy to put some makeup on. Though I had lost half of my eyebrows and eyelashes, I still managed to paint a decent brow and create the illusion I still had somewhat full lashes. It felt good. The makeup helped me feel a little more like a woman. My energy and strength waxed and waned throughout each round of treatment, but on the good days, I loved to wear my makeup and began wearing jeans and heels too. As I sat in my assigned seat in ODS every day, I also discovered online shopping, where I purchased several pairs of large, flashy earrings. I tried feathers, leather, and beads until I found ones that made me feel good. I began wearing them too. As the days went by, more people would stop me to compliment my bravery. And while I did not love that word in the context of how people cope with having cancer and treatment, I wondered whether my choice to do things that made me feel good was positively impacting others around me. I was definitely referred to as a badass more than once. I was beginning to feel more comfortable with my new look, and I suspected that coming to accept myself as I was might have been helping others too.

As I settled into the new me, I realized that the chemo had not ravaged my femininity. Rather, it had ravaged everything about me that was an illusion. It had stripped me down and delivered me back to basics. I had spent significant effort all my life to achieve acceptance, some of those years unknowingly, but who I had been underneath had always been a badass. I had spent my whole life stifling her, shaming her, and now, oddly enough, she could finally breathe. And though I so deeply feared that I would no longer be desirable, Marvin looked at me no differently. It was as though he did not see my sickness at all. I began to learn that the things I had feared most about losing my hair never actually came to pass because maybe, just maybe, my target audience should never have been anyone but me. It occurred to me that perhaps the people whose approval I so desperately sought were not the people whose support I wanted in the first place. I wondered if they would like the genuine me, but a split second later, decided it did not matter. On some level, I knew that as long as what I looked like on the outside was more important than who I was inside, I did not want to be desired by them anyway. Because who I was—who I *am*—is a strong, intelligent, ambitious badass. Even if everyone on the planet disliked me for those things, I would rather be a party of one and comfortable in my own company than ever betray myself again in a roomful of people who did not truly know me, or, worse, never actually wanted to.

All there was left to do from there was to rebuild. But this time would be different. All the experiences and happiness I had robbed myself of while trying to be someone I thought others would like more sat squarely in the center of my conscious mind, reminding me that while those efforts may have gotten me some results, the results were not happiness and self-fulfillment. Furthermore, there were now two young girls watching and learning from me, and I did not want to set the wrong example for them. No, I would not conform this time. I would not reference the women's handbook to desirable femininity. Instead, I would unapologetically be exactly who I wanted to be.

CHAPTER NINE
SELF-WORTH

The very last time I became a single woman, I was thirty-two. But that time was different. I had a one-year-old daughter. My first year as a single mom was the most challenging year of my life up to that point. Though I was surrounded by people who cared and wanted to help, the fact was, they could not. I felt alone. I felt ashamed. How could I have made it all the way into my thirties without being married or with a child, only to end up a single mom at thirty-two? The faces and voices of too many adults crept into my consciousness from the dark recesses of my memories. They said *We told you so. We told you all those years ago that you would be a disgrace, that you would not amount to anything, and here you are.*

I was still living up to my career expectations, and my daughter, Victoria, was one of the most ambitious toddlers I have ever known. She was only ten months old when she took her first steps, and she began kicking a soccer ball a month later. It was the beginning of an exhausting time in my life. The first time I took her to the beach after she started walking, she developed a fascination with seagulls. She showed no interest in playing with buckets or shovels on the beach. Nope! Instead, Victoria spent hours running up and down the shoreline chasing the birds. I was grateful to have friends with us. When one of us tired of running after her, we would tap someone else in for a shift. Though it was tiring, I loved that Victoria had such a zest for life!

I remember Victoria's first averse reaction to someone. It was just before she turned two years old. We were looking for a new place to live, and a townhouse rental had become available close to my workplace. I thought it would be an excellent place to settle to start our new life. Most exciting was the communal green space that would allow her to run and play with other kids—an option she had not previously had. After work one afternoon, I picked Victoria up from daycare, and we drove to the townhouse to meet the real estate agent renting it out on behalf of his clients. As soon as we walked through the front door, she ran down the hallway to explore. I had not experienced a place feeling right for a long time, and this place felt right. The agent tried to interact with Victoria when she ran back down the hallway toward us. She stopped dead in her tracks, stared at him and started fussing. He tried to coax her into shaking his hand, but she refused. I was stunned by her reaction. From the moment she was able, she had begun conversing with the world, so it was shocking to see her respond so unenthusiastically to someone. It sparked a "mama bear" reaction in me. The agent genuinely seemed nice, but Victoria's response gave me pause. So, I picked her up and plunked her on my hip for the remainder of our tour.

After dinner that day, I cleaned her up, put her to bed, and finally got to think on my own. I evaluated how I felt about Victoria's earlier reaction to the real estate agent. I followed several parenting websites, subscribed to parenting magazines and had read everything I could about parenting before becoming a parent and into the first year of her life. A repeating theme that came up was the instinct of children. Children are not yet tainted by the world's imposed beliefs, so their instinctive reactions are purer than those of adults. I believe there is a reason if a child reacts a certain way. I wondered what she had picked up on that I had not. I recounted our entire interaction that afternoon, and there were no red flags I could sense. I asked myself what I was missing. Nothing came to mind, which prompted the next question: Why? Why was I unable to detect what she had? It is an odd feeling when you realize that your own instinctive response may be broken, and you may not be able to see something right in front of you.

I could recount some occasions when I had missed warning flags, which had put me in precarious positions. However, I wondered how often I had been in the same kind of situation without understanding what was happening within me. I vowed to do everything I could to prevent the same thing from happening to my daughter. I wanted to help her know how to detect those who would hurt her before she ended up in situations like I had found myself in. I wanted her to grow up witnessing love, respect and true partnership. I refused to be a party to modelling that she should minimize her desires or her belief in herself to meet the traditional expectations of gender roles—the lesson we women so often hear about being polite to strangers and "not making a fuss." I vowed to teach her to pay attention to what her instincts told her about people. But how could I do that if I did not trust my own ability to assess others?

I recalled something I had been told not long before in a heated argument. *With so many failed relationships, maybe* you *are the problem, since the common denominator is you*. It was a callous statement meant to hurt me, and, at the time, it did hurt, but years later, I still wondered if it was true.

I continued to find myself in unhealthy relationships. Why did I keep dating the same type of man over and over? Three months of online dating had proven that who I was attracted to had not changed, which was not working for me. How was I supposed to stop that from happening? And why did I have higher expectations for my daughter than for myself? It was the first time in my life that I had taken a deep, introspective look at why I had made the relationship decisions I had. It was alarming to consider that this was not a random pattern but a result of some unknown function within me that said, “Yes! That person is right for you!” only to be disappointed and frantically picking up the pieces of my life again. Only now, it was not just my life that would be impacted. It was Victoria’s, too.

I have been a supporter and consumer of psychotherapy for many years. As a teenager, therapy helped me heal after my parents’ separation and gave me direction in my life. My first therapist was Larry Nisan. He was a kind and gentle man who made me feel safe. Larry was the reason I wanted to be a counsellor growing up. I looked up to him and wanted to help people the way he had helped me. There had been times throughout my life that I needed guidance, so I would call Larry. I was always confident he would steer me in the right direction.

So, naturally, I picked up the phone and dialled his office number. But this time, his wife, Christine Nisan, answered my call. She shared the news that Larry had passed away and that she had taken over his practice. I was sad to hear the news, as Larry had played a pivotal role in my life. The world had lost an exceptional human too soon. But I knew I would be safe in Christine’s hands, so I booked an appointment with her. When I sat down with her for my first session, I got straight to the point. I had two questions I needed answered:

1. Why do I keep picking the same type of man over and over?
2. How do I stop it from happening again?

Christine recommended a book called *Getting the Love You Want*, by Harville Hendrix, Ph.D. My ego turned its nose up at the title of the book. I did not want to be a woman desperately seeking men's attention. But looking back, I realized that I *did* want the attention of a man. My daughter was not getting any younger, and I wanted her to have a sibling who could also be a playmate one day. The clock was ticking! I stuffed my initial reaction down and gave the book a shot.

Reading through the first few chapters was one of the most enlightening experiences of my life. It was not a foreign concept to me that my upbringing might have impacted who I had become as an adult. But I had not spent much time thinking about how my upbringing would influence what I ultimately sought out in a partner or how it might positively or negatively impact our interactions.

In short, the book taught me about the neurological process of how we, as humans, subconsciously develop the "ideal" partner. We subconsciously build that person in our minds by observing the most impactful role models around us growing up. For better or worse, we recognize strong traits in them, which make up what we look for in others. But there is more to it than that. We also internalize those same characteristics, as we perceive that those strong traits are what will keep us safe. So, if we witness love and nurturing in those most influential role models, we will likely grow up to be loving and nurturing, and we will seek out the same in our partners. However, if we grow up witnessing and experiencing abuse, violence, and neglect, we will likely internalize these behaviours, and unconsciously seek them out in potential partners.

What's more, as we grow up, society tells us that certain behaviours are unacceptable, so if we internalize negative traits, we may come to feel shame about them and hide those parts of us. Sometimes we hide them so well, we do not even consciously know we have them.

This may be a lot to take in. I get it. I had to read pieces of the book repeatedly to digest what I had learned.

Ready to go on? Okay, stick with me here.

Now, imagine you have grown up watching adults communicate through yelling, and you also express yourself through yelling. You go to elementary school, and other kids or teachers chastise you for communicating in the only way you know how. Maybe you double down on that behaviour and are labelled a problem child, or maybe you suppress that characteristic because the pain of shame is too much to bear. Then you grow up to find someone you think is perfect for you, but eventually, you learn that they express themselves through yelling too. I thought back to all the times I had experienced this kind of thing. It began early in life.

My classmates and I were in grade six, and we were on a much-anticipated trip to Camp Wanakita, near Hamilton, Ontario. We were sitting in the dining hall one evening when the camp counsellors announced a competition. The table that left the least waste (i.e., ate the most) would win. On the menu were pork roast and vegetables. I rarely eat pork now, and you could be sure there was no chance I was putting pork fat in my mouth as a kid, and there was an abundance of it on my plate. It would not have mattered if a trip to Disneyland had been on the line! My cabinmates pressured me to finish all my food, but I pretended I did not hear them and ignored them when they insisted. Pushed far enough, I loudly proclaimed, "I'm not eating the fat. I don't care about the competition."

It was social suicide. My cabinmates and I rarely interacted for the remainder of the trip. That night, I lay in bed looking up at the dark ceiling and chastising myself for not eating what was on my plate. Not only had I raised my voice, but I let my team down as well. What was wrong with me? I felt ashamed.

Over the years, I repeatedly learned the lesson that people back away when others communicate abruptly or loudly. Eventually, I silenced myself, but that did not stop me from finding partners who chose the alternative—yelling.

In retrospect, what I never did was ask myself *why* I had reacted that way in the dining hall that night. Was it reasonable to pressure someone to eat something they did not want to? Was a boundary being violated? Granted, I could have clearly verbalized my boundary ("I don't care for pork, and I don't like fatty food,"), but setting boundaries was never encouraged or modelled in my home when I was growing up. It was not uncommon in the 1980s for parents to raise children with the overarching rule of "Do as I say, not as I do." The fatal flaw in such a rule is it prevents children from learning where and how to set their own boundaries. It takes away any autonomy and creates complacent humans who end up just waiting for instructions and often tolerating whatever life throws at them without protest.

The book Christine recommended helped me understand that those very things had been my experience. I recognized that I had reacted in the only way I could have on that trip. I also learned that I needed to hug my twelve-year-old self and tell her I had done the best I could with the knowledge I possessed at the time. The book also allowed me to reflect on how far I had come in learning to communicate effectively.

Those teachings answered the first question I had asked Christine: *Why do I pick the same type of man over and over?* I was selecting the same kind of man over and over because those men represented the unconscious ideal I had built as a young person. I also learned that when I engaged in those relationships, I found that the things I had spent so much time burying in myself were extremely challenging to tolerate in potential partners. I witnessed my "bad" behaviours mirrored in them, and all those years after my trip to Camp Wanakita, when my unspoken boundary was violated, I became that twelve-year-old girl again. I shrank from conflict, and when pushed beyond my ability to contain my shameful traits, I yelled. So when that person told me so callously, "Maybe it is your fault, since you are the common denominator," they were actually right. It *was* my doing.

At some point in our lives, we must shed the adolescent claim to innocence regardless of our upbringing and accept responsibility for who we are as adults. Reading that book was my reckoning. It was time to claim the power that had always resided within me.

That profound knowledge helped me understand that teaching my daughter to have higher standards than her mom was not about telling her what to avoid or seek out in others. It was about teaching her how to focus on what *she* wants from this life. To walk towards what she wants, not away from what she does not, just as I had done since the day those adults made their awful predictions about me. And the only way I could truly teach her was by owning that I am an imperfect work in progress, but that I am also worthy of love and grace. And that I deserve to be happy. She needed to see me make mistakes. She needed to see me fail. And then she needed to watch me demonstrate enough self-love to get back up and try again. She needed to see me put myself first. That was how she would learn self-love and expect better for herself. I would teach her that she is worthy by showing her that I, too, was worthy.

Returning home after my twenty-two-day stay in the hospital was challenging for several reasons. I had finished the first of my four phases of treatment—thirty-six consecutive days of chemotherapy. I took advantage of as much sleep and snuggles with my kids as much as possible during the three-week break before the next round of treatment would begin. My oncologist instructed me to rest as much as possible in preparation for the second phase. It was easy to rest when my fiancé was acting as mom and dad, and the house was lively with my kids. They were welcome distractions. But during the weekdays, between rounds of treatment, when the kids were in school and Marvin was at work, I could feel the mountains of laundry glaring at me with absolute judgment. I did not want to spend my precious, limited energy cleaning, but I did. It was like a reflex rather than a conscious decision. Resting was not something that came easily to me. I knew I should give myself a break, but the guilt of not doing enough—being enough—flooded in. You see, knowing you need to love yourself better does not necessarily mean you just magically start.

My energy was finite, and I did not have much of it given all my body had been through. I remember waking up one morning and deciding I wanted to have a normal day. I went into the bathroom, picked my favourite playlist and listened to music while I got ready for the day. While I brushed my teeth in front of my bathroom mirror, a song I loved started playing, and I started dancing. It was more of a shuffle than a full-on dance, but it was the only vigorous movement I had done in weeks. I managed to stay on my feet for a solid minute before blacking out. It was an essential lesson in energy consumption. Since my energy was so low, I needed to prioritize tasks strategically. By lunchtime, cognitively and emotionally, I was reduced to a toddler which meant I struggled with focus and experienced significant mood swings.

One morning, still valiantly trying to keep up with the household chores, I decided to tackle the super-judge-y laundry. It seemed necessary as I started, but I was grumpy by the time I flipped the second load. Forty-five minutes later, I found myself crouched in front of the dryer folding miniature socks together, with an excruciating pain in my knees, feeling absolutely livid, and wondering, "Why am I doing this?" Yet, I did it all *and* carried all the baskets up two flights of stairs.

When Marvin got home that night, I recounted the day's activities. In the passive-aggressive way I used to handle my feelings, I told him how exhausted I was, followed by my experience of doing the laundry that day. I finished by saying, "I do not know why I do this to myself."

He said, "Me either," in his calm and matter-of-fact way. Though I did not have enough energy to emote, my immediate reaction was hurt, followed closely by anger. I thought, "Well, who else will do it?" He could see my emotions shift and went on, "Nobody asked you to do the laundry."

On some logical level, I knew his statement was in no way intended to offend me, but to my ears, it sounded like, "This is not something I value about you." As the old, familiar panic sliced through my mind, I thought, *If doing laundry does not make me valuable, what does?*

THE REMAINING FOUR MONTHS OF IV CHEMOTHERAPY were a monotonous, "Groundhog Day" sort of experience. My family had implemented an action plan in the early days of treatment, and I was incredibly grateful for that. My dad had taken the first shift by being with me daily while I was in hospital, and Mom took over upon my release. She would drive me to and from the hospital nearly every day for four months for the remainder of IV treatment. She was also an incredible help to Marvin and me in managing our home and children.

The daily trips to the hospital were enough to drive anyone to insanity. As a creature of habit, I have always appreciated repetition, but sitting in ODS every day with sick people—*being* a sick person—was depressing on a level that only those who have been through it could understand. Shortly after treatment began each day, neither my mom nor I could stand the boredom, the waiting around, so we began making friends to pass the time. We created an impressively social atmosphere, despite how you might imagine a cancer ward to be. Often, my nurses had to wade through the IV poles of our new friends to reach me and stop the maddening beep of my infusion pump.

Two weeks before the end of IV treatment, I cracked. The emotional floodgates exploded open, and with it came a phenomenal amount of pain and grief. Nearly every day when I arrived at ODS, my nurse practitioner, Kristine, sat with me, and we talked about my health; we shared stories of our lives and joked. But on that day, she hugged me. She asked me what was wrong. I tried to tell her with any level of coherence that I was just tired. I was tired of being there every day and of my life being on pause. She offered me a private room that day to give me a reprieve from the social expectations I had created for myself. I declined her offer, even though I knew I needed the quiet. She settled for leaving me on the ward with the curtains drawn for privacy before giving me one last hug and moving on to her next patient. I appreciated the anonymity because I could not muster a smile, any more than I could stop the flow of my tears.

Finishing IV treatment was not the climactic conclusion we see in movies or social media. There was no bell; there were no claps or signs of congratulations. There was simply the beeping of my infusion pump, signalling the last time my PICC (peripherally inserted central catheter) line would ever be unhooked from my right arm again. After all, treatment was not truly over. After a break, I would begin the final and longest phase of treatment: maintenance. This phase would go on for two years with chemotherapy in pill form.

It seemed with IV treatment done, though, everyone expected life to go back to normal. Questions turned from "How are you doing?" to "When are you returning to work?" My family needed to get on with their own lives, so I was alone most days with my fragmented mind and beat-up body. Although the personal growth I had done before becoming sick told me I needed to prioritize myself better, I felt an acute need to step back into the world as a functioning adult. I began to question whether I should go back to work, and ultimately decided "Not yet." I was glad I'd made that decision, because my mental health completely deteriorated within days. I was depressed, angry, and sad. I would never say that self-regulation is my most impressive quality, but even so, this took me by surprise. It seemed I had utterly lost control of my emotions; I started having temper tantrums resembling a child going through the terrible twos. Though I was never diagnosed, I understood what I was experiencing was likely post-traumatic stress disorder, or PTSD. This is common, particularly in people who have experienced acute illness. Given how quickly I became ill and started treatment, there had been no time to feel. There was only action. But one way or the other, emotions need to come out, and despite my best efforts, now that I had little energy reserve, they were doing just that.

It was not long after that that I booked my first post-chemo counselling appointment. I had visited Natalie a few times before I was diagnosed. I was grateful that she and I already had an established professional relationship. It allowed us to bypass the "getting to know you" stuff, for which I could not spare the energy. She knew who I was before I was sick, and I was confident her prior knowledge would help guide me in this turbulent time.

I sat down in the waiting room once I arrived at her office. Only two other people were seated there with me. Natalie walked through the doorway and looked around, puzzled. It was as though she did not see me. It dawned on me that she did not recognize me. I popped out of my chair with a big smile and saw the disorientation hit her. She welcomed me, and we walked into her office together.

I spent much of the first appointment explaining how life had changed since the last time I had seen her. I explained the trauma of the events leading up to diagnosis and how I had made it just in the nick of time. I explained the treatment my body had endured and how I had felt useless through my recovery, like a dependent surrounded by people who relied on me to be more than that. Last, I explained the inner turmoil I felt about returning to work. Being asked so often when I would go back was making me feel that I should, though I knew I would not be ready to do so for quite some time. Yet, I felt this pressure, which in turn made me feel defensive. I also felt like I was robbing Marvin of the relationship that he deserved. I kept thinking to myself that this was not what he had signed up for (even though, of course, he reassured me as best as he could!). Thrown in the mix was a profound, visceral anger at how I had been dismissed and mistreated pre-diagnosis and even throughout treatment by some healthcare providers outside my care hospital.

I managed to maintain my composure through the telling of the story. In fact, reflecting on all the times I have told the story since, I do not recall crying often. But when Natalie asked how my kids were coping, I began to weep. The emotions were so consuming that I could feel them in the tips of my fingers, trying to force their way out. Speaking freely to someone who did not rely on me and would not judge me was a colossal relief. I sobbed through my words, explaining the things that contributed to the emotional overload.

Along with the physical pain I experienced daily, I told her, the battle to find solutions that would not lead to even more complications was exhausting and infuriating. I had developed a love-hate relationship with conventional medicine. On the one hand, I was grateful it had saved my life. On the other hand, I was resentful that the answer to every roadblock was more prescription drugs. Everything felt insurmountable. The emotional pain and frustration manifested into a palpable physical unease, making me want to claw my way out of my skin.

Natalie listened as I talked and cried, waiting until I was able to regain some composure. When I finally caught my breath, she moved us into a grounding exercise to teach me how to pull myself out of the spiralling darkness. She told me to plant both feet firmly on the ground as I sat on the couch, then to close my eyes and feel my breath. I became more aware of my body, which helped me get a grip. When I could regulate my breathing, she asked me a question that changed my life.

"Michelle, who are you without your titles?"

I was confused by the question and unable to evoke a response. I looked at her, perplexed. Then she said, "When you are not an employee, mom, or partner, who are you?"

Still, I did not have an answer, but she persisted: "What do you like to do when you are not fulfilling your roles? What do *you* enjoy doing?"

Grief for the life I had and lost washed over me. I could not answer her first question then, and I do not know whether I could have answered it before my life was upended, either. My initial assessment was that living with labels *is* life. The roles that I played were what made me who I was. They were what determined how I focused my attention at any given time—and, frankly, even who I was in those settings was nuanced. When I walked through the front doors of my place of employment, I was a badass relationship manager who advocated for her clients and wore thick armor. (It is debatable whether the armor was to protect me from the emotions of others or to keep mine locked inside.) When I was a partner to my spouse and mom to my kids, I was a master planner and teacher of life lessons. The concept of being without any of those titles left me feeling empty. Once I was no longer even a good patient at the hospital every day, I felt that there was nothing left of me. There was just a shell of who I had been.

Before I got sick, there had been infrequent occasions when I found myself not in one of my roles. On reflection, I realized that, usually, I had found myself either bored and anxious or inebriated on a dance floor during those times. Neither of those things was an option in my new reality. My emotional turmoil eliminated boredom, and we already knew how dancing was going—and I loved myself well enough not to hinder my progress by polluting my body during that time.

Natalie left me with those questions as homework. Who was Michelle Burleigh, and what did she enjoy doing all by herself?

It is hard to say how long it took to work through her questions; during those days, it was challenging for me to discern the passage of time. One day, though, it clicked. It just made sense. I understood what Natalie had been driving at, and it caused a cascading reaction that led to the most significant mindset shift I have ever experienced.

Our society values the roles we play, *not* who we are. I do not believe this is an intentional or malicious tendency. For whatever reason, it just is. Think about times when we meet new people. Nearly without fail, one of the first questions we ask each other is about our employment. We ask, *So what do you do?* When we answer that question or any variation of it, we do not respond with, *I garden*, or *I like to play volleyball*. Instead, we tell people what our job is. We tell people about our families. We do not tell them what makes us happy or what makes us who we are. Can you imagine if someone was asked, "What do you do?" and that person shared that on Saturday mornings, they like to play air guitar to The Backyardigans with their four-year-old child?

In the same way that the first question we ask adults is about their work, our first question to children is often, "What do you want to be when you grow up?" I've never heard a child answer that question with a simple statement like, "To be happy," and that is certainly not the answer we adults are looking for.

I had fallen victim to the same rules and had internalized them so deeply that it took weeks for me to even understand Natalie's question. But regardless of social norms or conversational etiquette, I understood that *I* had put all my worth into the roles I played. And so, I had worked myself nearly to death at various points in my life to achieve the respect that I believed would surely come with perfecting them. Perfectionism had become a toxic focal point for me, as I believed that not just achieving but *over*-achieving in any of my roles would make me worthy. I thought perfection would validate my existence, and I took pride in striving for it and receiving praise for it. Compounding this problem, I also held everyone else to the same standards. I thought back to all the times I'd needed the cooperation of someone at work to complete a task and had been disappointed, annoyed and impatient because they did not prioritize things the way I would have. In retrospect, I saw that this was a significant flaw that had sometimes held me back and had also damaged relationships.

The laundry meltdown I'd had while I was on the break between the first and second rounds of treatment came back to me. A part of me believed being sick was not an excuse to let the laundry slip. I was consciously aware that was an unhealthy thought pattern but lacked the mental strength to combat it. More dangerously, I fully believed that if I was not physically well enough to do it, my partner should. It became clear that my need for perfection was not reasonable and, at times, had been detrimental to my health—and to the health of my relationship. I knew that was a block of work I needed to focus on.

In addition, it was also unfair of me to hold my partner to impossible standards, and I was grateful to have fleshed it out. Marvin had stepped up to the plate and supported our family in the best way he knew how through the worst time of our lives, and he deserved more credit than I was giving him. I knew that most of the time, of course, but occasionally my unhealthy beliefs stood in the way of that knowing. Acquiring a greater self-awareness helped me keep that knowledge front and center as I began unlearning toxic behaviours and relearning new healthy ones. I even wondered, *What is the worst that could happen if the laundry piles up?* It was a step in the right direction to dismantling my perfectionism and my need for control.

As a people pleaser, I felt I needed to be liked. I felt my value was in doing for others, but I was never happy. I constantly over-extended myself, ignoring my needs, which always led to resentment. People pleasers do not do things because we want to; we do things because we think we *need* to, and the solution to fix that seems so simple. In fact, Marvin had said as much—*Just stop doing it.*

Recognizing that, at thirty-seven years old, I did not have any healthy personal interests and had never truly taken care of my needs made losing the life I had had before cancer a little easier to bear. With this new knowledge, I realized that in those times when I'd actually had free time to myself, my behaviours were not self-loving. They were rebellious and self-destructive. I drank too much, ate poorly and didn't sleep enough. I had spent the better part of my adult years insisting I was not a victim, but I had been, and my poor behaviour had not improved things. Nor had measuring my value against the roles that I played. I knew it was time to turn over a new leaf. It was time to get reacquainted with myself, to take responsibility for myself and prioritize myself. It was time to let the past go and to recognize that as a grown woman, there was no one for me to rebel against.

Instead, I decided to explore what might truly make me happy. I decided to work on feeling worthy just because I am a living, breathing human, and I doubled down on my commitment to live the life I had always wanted to live but had not dared enact. I re-affirmed that I would live life on my own terms. I would no longer feel shame about how I chose to spend my time because I had learned the hard lesson that, when my time expires, there will be no more chances and the only person I will have to answer to is myself.

The irony was that for so long, I had thought that motherhood meant putting my children first. But in reality, I could not be the mother I wanted to be to my girls if I was resentful of always back-burnering myself. So, I made the decision that my needs would come first. That does not mean that I would not go to the ends of the earth to support and protect my children. It simply meant that I needed to put my love for myself first. Over time, this resolve grew more potent, and as it did, my anger dissipated, and I began to move towards inner peace.

I could never have imagined how it would change my life.

CHAPTER TEN

THE FIVE STEPS TO SELF-ACTIVATION

Before I go on, it is important to note that the events of 2020 through 2022 have had a terribly negative impact on the world. North America is no exception. Besides the obvious, it has created an undeniable divide among people. No matter a person's personal choices, we have observed the unrelenting need for people to be right, like the absolutes mentioned earlier. This leaves a gaping hole in the space where curiosity and exploration should be. When we hear someone express an opinion, we have a tendency to disagree if it does not suit our narrative. Instead of seeking to understand, or at the very least respect that someone thinks differently than we do, we close the door on conversation, defend our position and, in some cases, even launch global attacks on each other.

While I believe it is important to have beliefs and values to live by, I also believe that we need to be curious in order to grow. If we are unable to be flexible and curious, we are unable to progress. This demand for absolutes is stunting our ability to be inquisitive about both ourselves and others, and it is preventing us from being compassionate and empathetic with each other. So, I implore you to read on with an open heart and inquisitive mind.

I, LIKE MANY SURVIVORS, HAVE BEEN PROPELLED BY THE myriad of emotional, psychological and physical challenges I have faced since my diagnosis. As a former control freak, I know now that losing complete control of our lives can either break us or teach us to grow—not so different from what the rest of the world has experienced due to the COVID-19 pandemic.

In my own case, in a futile attempt to hold on to control of my life, I fought like a lioness protecting her cubs. But under the circumstances, like it or not, my control was gone. It was a distressing feeling, but each time I found myself in emotional upheaval for seemingly no reason and crying in front of the television, I became more curious about why I felt embarrassed to be doing so. Why would I feel ashamed of being emotional? Over time I began to accept that this is fundamentally what makes us human. And while corporate North America has worked hard to strip us of that —and I had bought into it—you simply can not deprive the body of emotions any more than you can remove its heart. So, rather than fighting my feelings each time I felt emotional, I allowed them to come and go. The truly life-changing epiphany was the realization that we are fractured when we deny our emotions. But when we stop fighting them and instead invite them, we become whole again. And that meant that after decades of "*I could never*," I was more interested in exploring what made me happy and how I felt. I was finally able to visualize smashing the pretty little box I had been living in all my life.

It meant that, unbeknownst to me, I had just unlocked the possibility of reaching my true potential. I wanted to start down that path by, first of all, empowering Canadians to advocate for themselves in healthcare. As I slowly climbed out of that pretty little box, one part of me told myself that there was no place for me in healthcare, that I had no business in that space. But a quieter voice, one that was a little shaky, a little unsure, said *What if?* And the first step in choosing to pursue that goal was to begin living in a constant state of disruption. In other words, I would start living my life *actively seeking discomfort* to nurture that quieter inner voice. Like a good workout, to build muscle, you must work what you have almost to the point of injury and then let it heal. And when the cycle is complete, and you start to feel comfortable with the new discovery, realization or skill, it's time to start questioning what you can do to grow beyond that point. Why? Because we simply are not designed to stay the same. Stagnancy is where disease develops. And frankly, we can't achieve our wildest dreams without developing new skills and confidence.

One of the hopeful side effects of the Covid-19 pandemic has been the injection of emotion back into business. So many people have spent their careers shoving feelings down—enduring excruciating emotional pain in silence to maintain the appearance of professionalism even when they have experienced devastating loss and dire circumstances, yet, I, myself have witnesses senior leaders bare their stories of struggle and sadness during the darkest days of the pandemic. It appeared to be the breaking point for many and the subsequent rush of humanity flooding back into some corporate businesses who now seem to recognize that we all have a personal story and it's better to support each other in hard times. It truly is a beautiful thing to behold kindness and compassion in business, and I, for one, believe that the opportunities for creativity and innovation are endless in the presence of such mutual support. But I digress.

Illness takes so much from us: our privacy, bodily autonomy and dignity. Sometimes it leaves us with scars or missing body parts, or maybe a body that does not work as it used to. Study after study tells us physical illness can also cause acute and chronic mental health issues. While some degree of all that is true for all of us who experience illness, sometimes that same illness leaves us with gifts too. Having leukemia left me with many things. Among them was the knowledge that my life could end at any moment. This begged the question: Would I believe that I had lived the life I wanted to live if I were gone tomorrow?

I knew that the answer was no. In fact, I had no appreciation for how crucial that question was until the day I was admitted to the hospital, unsure whether I would live to see tomorrow. I had accomplished some things, to be certain, but I had not accomplished nearly as much as I believed that I still could. Cancer had introduced me to the most critical crossroads of my life and, after I was out of the woods, it gave me two options: to continue doing what I had always done, or to live the life I never had the courage to live before. The choice was simple. There was no going back.

I feel deeply for my fellow survivors who grieve the loss of who they were before cancer, though I cannot claim to relate. I imagine their pain stems from losing things about themselves that they once loved—their feeling of invincibility, their energy, a pain-free, scar-free, carefree existence. For me, life had already beat me around enough that I did not feel invincible to begin with. I had already suffered physical pain thanks to years of chronic back pain, and I had spent years trying to claw my way out of trauma responses. So the grief I have experienced after cancer goes only as far as the burden of knowing things that are hard to know. Generally speaking, most people who have never experienced an existential crisis do not walk about wondering if today is the day it all ends for them. I long for a life that's more oblivious, less informed. I envy those who can socialize with friends and have a glass of wine without worrying whether they have caused some intestinal disease, or who can lie on a beach in the sun without worrying whether they have increased their risk of melanoma.

It is the blissful ignorance I miss, but the grief never stays long because who I was before that knowing was paralyzed, willfully ignorant, and stagnant. The more time that passed, the less I could relate to her, and I do not miss her now.

I was, and remain, fully aware that we do not transform our lives overnight, though I did know that transformation was the goal. It is one thing to discover a new desire and it's a completely different thing to commit to it. I had chosen to prioritize my own well-being, and the more I held that in my conscious mind, the more I wanted to experience the possibilities—inner peace, total self-devotion, and true happiness. And the more I wanted to share that possibility with others.

I first had to acknowledge that my mental barriers existed in the first place because I had put them there. Yes, I could analyze the intentionality or lack thereof in the first place if time was endless and energy infinite, but I had learned to focus only on the things that would bring me what I wanted from this life, and besides, finger-pointing would serve no one. Instead, I focused solely on what I needed to focus on to move forward. I knew in my bones that I had been given a second chance at life for a purpose. I had spent most of my life thinking meditation, gratitude, and fate were nonsense, but I could not shake the belief that I am still here for a reason.

Having been through such a horrific experience leading up to diagnosis, I could not help but ask myself how many people in my situation would have just gone back home or returned to work that day after being invalidated by medical professionals the way I was. I could not help but wonder how many people in my exact same situation, deemed too young for cancer, not sick-looking enough, or too assertive for the fragile ego of an administrative professional, have lost their lives because they would not, or could not, fight for themselves. I wondered how many people—women, in particular—had been taught that to speak up was unladylike or impolite. While I worked on healing my own trauma and strengthening my relationship with myself, I also began thinking about how I could support other Canadians entering the healthcare system. And I realized that this was my calling.

I knew coming to terms with my past and learning to be kinder to myself would not be an easy task. It was not enough to know that the mental barriers were there. I also needed to work on breaking them down. It would require new techniques and fortitude. I needed to feed that shaky little voice with confidence and strength, and doing so would require ripping apart the synaptic pathways that told me I was incapable of making that kind of change and rebuilding them to tell me that I could do *anything* I put my mind to.

Through trial and error, I developed a personal strategy for how to work through the things that had been holding me back and, more importantly, how to move forward so I could start working towards my goals. It was not enough to tell myself I wanted to live the rest of my life on my own terms. I wanted to help others too, and achieving that goal meant I would need two things I had not had much of: courage and discipline.

Self-activation was always challenging because my mental barriers told me I could not achieve whatever task was of interest, that I would hurt myself, I would look silly, or people would judge me. It was never that I didn't want to try new things, it was just that fear held me back. The strategy I created for myself really helped me to push through some of the most difficult challenges: strengthening my mental health, making career decisions, parenting, improving relationships with others, taking personal accountability for my actions and feelings and, if you can believe it, learning how to play. The strategy consists of five steps:

1. Acknowledge that anxiety is rooted in fear.
2. Identify what is within our control.
3. Recognize the potential consequences of acting, or not.
4. Be accountable.
5. Accepting the outcome, come what may.

By following this process, no matter what situation I run into, I can think clearly and make decisions based on what I know in my heart is right for me, rather than acting (or not) on fear or the subconscious desire to prove myself. That does not mean it is always comfortable. I assure you, it is not. Keeping these steps in mind when I'm faced with a decision has taught me that (presuming my morals, ethics, and personal safety are not compromised) I can just do things scared. Using this methodology has supported me through a significant mental shift. It has allowed me to live a more courageous life that is not only inline with the life goals I have set for myself but is carried out on no one's terms but my own.

Let's take a look in greater detail at each step.

ACKNOWLEDGE THAT ANXIETY IS ROOTED IN FEAR

In the early days of my diagnosis, when I was futilely still trying to gain control of an uncontrollable situation, we can agree that in such a heightened emotional state, some of my thoughts and actions were erratic. After all, my oncologist was not my personal answering service despite how many questions I wanted to ask. Instead, I asked my medical team where I could find information about my diagnosis and what to expect with treatment. They pointed me in the direction of the many pamphlets they had tucked neatly in a box hung on the wall of the patient lounge. The staff encouraged me to read those materials and, with nothing but good intention, advised me to avoid social media. When I asked why, the nurse explained that there is a lot of misinformation to be found there, and it does not help anybody—in fact, some of it can be downright harmful.

I read through the pamphlets, but I did not feel any less afraid or uncertain. So, despite the nurses' advice, I went online in search of comfort and belonging. While I agree there is a lot of scary, anxiety producing things that appear in online search engines, I found several helpful resources on social media. I began following an ever-growing roster of cancer and mental health accounts that spoke to the awakening of the psyche, healing and growing into our own truths. I found that although not everything out there was for me, I could easily manage that in two different ways. First, if I came across disturbing content that did not apply to me, I could simply block those posts and accounts. Second, sometimes it was not immediately obvious whether content applied to me or not, so I would keep reading and spend time contemplating if that content was right for me. Then I would make the decision to continue following, or not.

Recognizing that I had a lot of de-programming to do, I ran headlong into countless opportunities to challenge my thoughts and feelings. If I ultimately decided that certain things applied to me and there was some sort of reckoning to be had there, I would sit with the information as long as I needed to learn the lesson. If it did not apply to me, I could accept that those things were not my truth and keep searching. Once in a while, I found something that immediately resonated with me. To my own surprise, years later, I have found that social media has been directly responsible for some of my most life-changing revelations. Simply put, social media is what we make of it. To some nurses, it was a scary place they feared would misguide their patients, and I could see how that would be true for some. For me, it was what I needed to find connection.

One of the most impactful quotes I came across early in my journey of healing was by the ancient Chinese philosopher Lao Tzu. He said, "If you are depressed you are living in the past. If you are anxious you are living in the future. If you are at peace you are living in the present." I suspect that my psychotherapist had already been working towards helping me come to this realization during our sessions. However, I had difficulty relating my anxious behaviour to fear. I believed that fear was weakness, and after all I had been through and survived, experience had taught me that vulnerability was dangerous.

What I find so terribly unfortunate is how often adults justify the trauma of children by saying "The kids will be fine," or "Kids are so resilient." I suppose the accuracy of such a statement depends on a person's perception of "fine." Some children appear to shake off traumatic events and then internalize them, never expressing fearful emotions because the adults around them have led them to believe fear is a sign of weakness; to an adult who doesn't look deeper than that, those kids will surely seem "fine."

Perhaps I, too, had looked more or less "fine" as a child and young adult. But I was a thirty-seven-year-old woman reading a quote on my phone after going through the most horrific experience of my life, aware that there was a connection but unable to put coherent words together to describe it. I had never allowed myself to express fear or be labelled a victim. Instead, I had always pushed through, buried my feelings and devised elaborate plans to prevent myself from ever ending up in similar situations again. My childhood trauma had undoubtedly taken a toll on me, and refusing to deal with it properly had come at a cost. I still carried a phenomenal amount of anxiety. Was I fine? According to Dr. Gabor Maté, a psychologist, physician and author of the book *When The Body Says No: The Hidden Cost of Stress*, I was not fine. In fact, in that book, he directly addresses how our emotional state may contribute to the onset of several diseases, including leukemia.

In the early days after my diagnosis, the perilousness of my situation forced me to be in the present. In the crudest way. I learned, in no uncertain terms, that planning every minute detail of my life to avoid disaster was pointless. My habitual fear response to the unknown had certainly not prevented me from ending up in my situation. But it *had* prevented me from living to the fullest.

I reflected on the pressure I felt to return to work. I asked myself who was pressuring me to go back. I knew it was not my employer because I had already called them and tried to initiate a conversation about going back, and they had told me to cool my jets. Was this another instance of me putting undue pressure on myself to fulfill another role, or maybe defending myself against an unlikely outcome—that they would fire me for taking advantage of them? I suspected the answer was "yes" and "yes." I sat with that uncomfortable feeling. I did not try to push it down, lock it in a box or deny it. I allowed myself to feel it as long as I needed to.

I had always felt a lot of pride in my career. I had worked extremely hard to get where I was, and my reputation meant a lot to me, but I do not think I realized that I had already done the hard work and was respected as a high-performing professional. I no longer needed to prove myself. I had done that, and at a time when I needed to focus on myself, those with whom I had established trust and respect supported me in return. That was a pivotal shift in mindset for me, and it caused a cascade of questions about how my negative thoughts were influencing my health, anxiety levels and work habits. What purpose did it serve me to armor up for something that was unlikely? And what had caused the near instantaneous shift from *Keep sending me work!* to *I'm going to quit my job!*

I was so worked up and held such unnecessary hostility towards my employer—revolving around a fabricated future event. Even more confusing were my feelings of ambivalence towards losing my job. I enjoyed my job, and the perks that came along with it but I wondered how high the cost would be to my personal well-being. Between the time of my admission to hospital and when I returned to work, I had had the time to work through those thoughts and feelings only to discover that fear was the underlying emotion; fear of losing my job, fear of feeling overwhelmed if I worked through those days in the hospital, fear at the very idea that I was willing to do so. I had come to know in my logical mind that maintaining my wellbeing would relate more to my being able to set and maintain work-life boundaries. So after months of working through intense thoughts and feelings, I accepted that the solution was not to run away—to swear off employment—but to develop the personal strength to decide what the right balance was for me and to trust my employer to support the healthy choices of its people. It required me to acknowledge that it was I, not my employer, who was creating my anxiety by limiting my thoughts and beliefs about myself and my ability to set healthy boundaries. And when I returned to work nearly three years later, they welcomed me with open arms and asked how they could support me. Unlike before, had I not had the support that I did, had I re-entered the business feeling that it wasn't right for me, I also had the confidence that I would do what needed to be done to manage my wellbeing and happiness.

I realize that circumstances vary for others who have found themselves in similar situations, and I feel deeply for those who are not so fortunate. But having had the time to work through it all, I accepted the kindness and support offered to me and moved back into my corporate life with gratitude and excitement, and also with the freedom of mind to prioritize the things I had come to love outside of corporate life.

If we look at a simple example of how anxiety can impact our lives, we can easily see that it serves no good purpose at all. Let's use learning how to ride a bike. Bike riding serves a plethora of purposes. Kids do it for fun, many adults do it for exercise, and some of us even do it as a means of commuting. Bike rides have contributed to some of my fondest memories with my kids.

Now, for a moment, imagine a world where no one learned to ride a bike because they were afraid to fall.

Anxiety is insidious. The irony is, we think it protects us, but it does not. It robs us of possibilities—joy, fun, learning, growth; the list goes on. It disguises itself as a remedy for pain, all while it paralyzes us. But what if, instead of worrying about what might come, we decided instead to believe in ourselves so wildly that there was no room left to fear the future? What if our vision of the future we want was so steadfast that no amount of worrying, criticism or roadblocks could stop us from achieving it?

Once we recognize that our anxiety is rooted in fear of outcomes we can not possibly forecast, we have the power to focus our energy and attention on our dreams. We can then make different decisions that will support us in the steps required to get there.

IDENTIFY WHAT IS WITHIN OUR CONTROL

Understanding that anxiety is rooted in fear, typically of the future, allowed me to view differently things like uncertainty, insecurity, and even that icky feeling we get when faced with an uncomfortable or unusual situation. I got better at recognizing that those feelings serve a purpose, and rather than avoiding them or trying to control them, I leaned into the discomfort. Those feelings meant that there was something for me to unpack and explore, and possibly something to learn about myself. For example, say I am speaking with someone who is making me feel uncomfortable. The first thing I can do is ask myself what about the interaction is making me feel uncomfortable. Am I being triggered in some way? For example, is that person being disrespectful or unkind?

Let's say that I've determined that that person is, indeed, speaking to me in an unkind way. My next step is to determine what is within my control. Can I make that person be kind? No, I can't, but I can do several other things that are within my control. I could inform them that I dislike the way I'm being spoken to and ask them to be kind, or I could let them know I will discontinue the conversation if I continue to feel that way, or I could just leave. All three of these possible outcomes would be fully within my control, and would also ensure I maintain my own integrity.

In the days and weeks following the completion of IV chemotherapy, I struggled with how much strength I had lost. I thought back to my childhood. I was only twelve years old when doctors identified structural problems with my body. I suffered from chronic pain for many years, on into my adulthood. Only a few years before I landed in the hospital, I had finally started getting serious about my physical health and had begun lifting weights, cycling, and doing things to strengthen my body. I had worked incredibly hard to get strong, and through that hard work and dedication I had lived a handful of years relieved of pain.

Now, though, I struggled to accept how much work it would require to get back there. I wanted to get back to the gym. I wanted to lift weights. I wanted to run. I could not stand running prior to falling ill, yet as soon as I finished IV treatment, it's all I wanted to do. But I knew I couldn't, and it made me angry. I spent some time sunk in self-pity, before shaking it off and reminding myself it wouldn't help me. So, rather than focus on the things I could not do, I looked at what was feasible given my physical, post-chemo condition. I began walking.

On the first day, I was devastated to learn that after only twenty minutes, I felt dizzy and faint and had to go back home. My knees and ankles were on fire, so I iced them and took a nap. But I was determined: every single day from that day forward, if I had enough energy, I walked. I suffered from constant swelling and inflammation, but given I still had two years left of maintenance therapy, I knew that would not change anytime soon. Preventing the swelling and inflammation was out of my control. But I could manage it by icing, elevating my legs and permitting myself to rest when needed. Eventually, twenty minutes turned to twenty-one, twenty-two, and then twenty-five minutes. Within six weeks, I could walk three kilometers at a slow pace. It took far longer than it would have before, but it was progress. Within a few weeks after that, the occasions when I required a nap during the day also lessened. My energy and strength had begun improving.

As I worked on identifying my anxiety triggers and focused on regaining strength, I noticed that my attention began to shift. While on my walks, I noticed birds, plants and bugs I had never seen before. I marvelled at the beauty of a single dewdrop that had fallen on a leaf. I could not imagine that such beauty had not previously existed, but why had I not seen these things before?

With curiosity and kindness, I focused on how I felt inside while I walked. I often walked listening to music. I had spent my whole life preferring loud, vibrant music, but when I forgot my headphones, I noticed something new: I felt at peace. It occurred to me that I could not recall a time in my life when I had enjoyed the silence, but now I relished the stillness, broken on some days only by the chirping of the birds on the tree-covered trails near home.

I remember walking past a car one morning. I turned my head to look at it and caught my reflection in the glass. I was shocked by the shape of my mouth, which formed a smile. I could plainly see what I felt inside as I observed the upward slant of my mouth: contentment. I also noticed that the chaos in my head—the busy, anxious voices and the plans I automatically concocted just in case something catastrophic occurred—were gone. I was just walking, seeing the beauty around me, hearing the sounds of the summer, expressing love for my body by moving it and expressing love for my mental health by allowing myself to enjoy the moment.

No matter the circumstances life throws at us, we can choose how we want to approach it. We can armor up and prepare for the worst, or we can allow ourselves to assess what is truly in our control, focus on that, and let the rest go. If we allow ourselves the latter, we free up our energy and attention to experience in high definition the best of what life has to offer.

RECOGNIZE THE POTENTIAL CONSEQUENCES OF ACTING ... OR NOT

By now, we have determined that what holds us back from living our dreams is anxiety—the fear of the unknown, or possibly better put, the fear of all the unlikely scenarios that will likely never befall us. We've also thought through what is within our control and what is not and decided we will focus only on what is within our control. But determining these things when learning to rewire our brains is not enough. We may require some additional encouragement.

This process step is related to determining the payoff of acting and, inversely, the cost of choosing not to. Within mere hours of landing in the hospital, I felt an overwhelming sense of frustration, even disgust, at how I had limited myself throughout my life. Time after time, I chose not to act because of unforeseen dangers. If I stayed put, I'd always told myself, there would be no danger. I thought back to all the times I had missed out on adventure because I was afraid to travel, try a new sport, or ask a challenging question. I thought of how many jobs I had stayed in, despite poor treatment, because I did not know what to expect elsewhere. And when the knowing deep inside me had screamed at me to act, I would soothe it by telling myself there was always a next time. I was disappointed in myself for robbing myself of knowledge and experiences, and I began to wonder what would have happened if I had instead prioritized determining the cost of *not* acting. But as we've learned, regret is a waste of energy. Instead, I familiarized myself with the feeling of knowing I had missed out, and resolved never to feel that way again.

The day that I sat down with my oncologist and heard that I might not live through the first ten days of treatment was when I learned exactly what it truly costs to be stagnant, comfortable. I also learned what there is to truly be afraid of: never having the opportunity for a next time. It is every missed opportunity to enrich my life and bring myself joy. I realized that I wanted to do more things that made me smile. I wanted to push myself out of the constant worry of the unknown.

Ultimately, we can waste our energy thinking about all the potential consequences of doing something, but we will never know the outcome until we get there. However, it requires significantly less energy to consider the cost of *not* acting. For example, when choosing whether or not to learn a new language, the outcome of saying "no thanks" is not simply that you will never be able to speak that language, it's also that you'll never be able to converse with those who speak it, and you'll have a hard time navigating in countries or cultures where it is the predominant language. If you choose not to get on a stage and talk to an audience, you cannot easily forecast the long-term benefits of making that choice, but you do know that you will limit yourself to jobs that do not require public speaking. For some people that might not be an issue, but maybe your dream job requires that skill and you never go for it because you won't allow yourself to try.

You can choose not to act, but when you do, make sure you understand what it will cost.

By challenging ourselves to really think about why we make the decisions we do, we can consider whether the decisions we make are truly in our best interest or if we are simply insulating ourselves from discomfort. If we go back to the example of learning how to ride a bike, the old me might have chosen not to get on the bike. I might have told myself I could hurt myself by falling, maybe even break a bone. But what would saying "no" have cost me? In retrospect, it would have cost me some of my favorite life memories. Riding bikes with my kids would never have been an option, and the thought makes me sad.

We focus so much time and effort on accumulating money and material things. But the most valuable things we acquire in life are the memories that make us smile, and frankly, they are the only things we get to take with us when we leave this life. So, be sure to weigh the risk versus benefit of choosing to act, or not.

BE ACCOUNTABLE

Just because we decide that doing something is a good idea, just because we've spent the time and effort to deconstruct the mental barriers that make us think we do not want to do something, does not mean we will act. I cannot say why, but I used to have this perception that growth, since it's a natural part of life, would be easy, that it would feel comfortable. I could not have been more wrong about that. If most of us recall some of our earliest memories of what growing up was like, we know that it is not easy. When we learn to walk, we inevitably fall. Sometimes we end up with cuts and bruises. And when we master gravity and can stand on our two feet, we try to run and again, we fall.

Even when we are doing nothing at all, our bodies grow so fast at times that we experience growing pains. Our bones, muscles and ligaments stretch so fast they hurt. I have distinct memories of sitting on the floor of my grandparents' living room with a hot water bottle across my legs, crying because they hurt so bad. My point is that growth is natural and sometimes it hurts.

The term 'comfort zone', in and of itself, is a contradiction. We believe we are safe and protected in this state. We are comforted by the belief that it is not harmful and we can be at ease. There are periods when this may be true. One's comfort zone can be a great resting place when we have already been through change and need rest, but staying there too long is unequivocally harmful—and the worst part is, we may not even know we're doing it. Even as I write this, I can feel the work I still need to do in my own thought patterns. A part of my brain wants me to type that my comfort zone feels good, but if I think back to times when I was in my comfort zone, it was not really a *good* feeling. It was simply *familiar*.

What's more, I felt stuck, and in some of those times, I was even being abused. So, no, I would not say that my comfort zone has always felt good, but I can say that it has always felt familiar. And depending on your life experiences, familiar does not necessarily equate to good or safe.

Our comfort zone discourages us from progressing because, from within it, progress *feels* counterintuitive. On some level, we know that growth is hard, uncomfortable and sometimes even painful. Growth can force us to face things that we have suppressed in order to survive. So, even if we acknowledge that doing something —taking a step or revealing a truth that must be spoken, for example—is the right thing to do, it does not mean we will.

There is **never** going to come a time when we feel comfortable doing things that feels counterintuitive. And the longer we wait, the greater the chances that life-changing opportunities will pass us by. Remember that anxiety causes fear of the future (or, as Lao Tzu would say, it *is* fear of the future), that some things are in our control and some things are not, and that there is always a cost/benefit ratio we must consider. So, if there is something I have already decided I want to do, but I am still not taking action, I have to ask myself what is holding me back.

Sometimes we must acknowledge that there are unconscious factors at play. These can and do trick us into believing our comfort zone is where we should be, and as I said earlier, that may be true at times. But if we want active growth, achievement and success, we must combat that feeling. As life has taught me, once an opportunity passes, we may never again get the chance to make a different choice.

Procrastination is the worst enemy of progress. It robs us of the opportunity to best prepare ourselves for change. When something feels uncomfortable we can always find an excuse not to do it or to put it off a little longer. We tell ourselves we have enough time, or that there are other priorities, but the reality is we *always* have time for the things we choose to prioritize. We need to recognize that the resistance we feel is just our subconscious telling us that stepping forward may cause discomfort. That discomfort could be speculation that others may be disappointed in us. It could be that we are acting against societal expectations and do not want to be judged. But none of that matters. At the end of the day, the only two things that matter are that we are true to ourselves, and that we are not intentionally hurting others.

Giving ourselves as much time as possible to prepare before we make decisions will help us manage those uncomfortable feelings and prevent further feelings of being overwhelmed. For example, if we are going to a job interview for an exciting opportunity and feel nervous, preparing what we want to say and practising with a friend or in front of a mirror will help manage nerves. If we are giving a speech and are afraid to speak in front of an audience, rehearsing the talk will help us feel more confident when we hit the stage. If we are having conflict with someone we care about, and we are uncomfortable voicing our truth, spending time in advance to focus on what is important to us, and maybe even practising in the mirror will help keep things on track if it gets tense.

Sometimes, though, even after putting all our effort into preparing, it will still just be uncomfortable. But as long as we act within our morals, ethics and boundaries, it is perfectly okay to feel that way. Do it anyway. Do it scared. Just do it.

ACCEPT THE OUTCOME, COME WHAT MAY

At this point in the process, we have completed the heavy mental lifting. Give yourself a pat on the back and be proud that you have held yourself accountable and taken action. This step will help break the pattern of stewing in utter anxiety, waiting for the other shoe to drop.

For those who struggle with anxiety, this process step is critical to helping ourselves enjoy the journey to our goal as much as possible. Even if we have achieved self-activation, remembering that change takes time, we may question ourselves every moment along the way and criticize our every step. This may lead us to ask if it was worth it, even with a desirable outcome, because the toll of the stress can be debilitating. As we already know, stressing about things gets us absolutely nowhere, so we must decide whether we are going to waste precious energy on that, or whether we are simply going to accept what may come.

No matter whether we choose to act or not, there will always be consequences, but if we know that we have done the best we can to effect the outcome we desire and we know that we have acted with absolute integrity, there is nothing more to do but focus on what is happening right now. We have honored ourselves by acknowledging our truth and going for it. While there are always consequences, whether they be positive or negative, there is no failure because we gave ourselves the opportunity to learn a little bit more than we knew before. The only actual failure is giving up. If it is worth fighting for, fight for it. Failure is an opportunity to learn and do better next time.

CONCLUSION
LIVING AUDACIOUSLY

Learning to live with intentionality was and remains deeply personal work. I am very grateful to have had the time and space to do so much of that work. In the years after my cancer diagnosis, I continued to question my thoughts and feelings about nearly everything, particularly when I felt resistance in my mind or body. I needed to understand why I felt the things I did. Were they grounded in a former belief that no longer served me, or were they a result of my gut instinct telling me there was, in fact, a reason to pay attention?

Over time, the line between those two things grew solid, with little room for questioning. I began to drown out the background noise of the world bickering about this or that and began to trust my feelings and make decisions based on them.

The evolution I experienced in the years following my diagnosis was immense. By using my new skills and the process of self-activation I have been able to imagine and put into action things I could never have dreamed possible. I am happier in my life and actively pursuing things that bring me fulfillment and joy. I have clear boundaries that I exercise as often as necessary, and with kindness.

I am a better parent and wife. I have fun new hobbies that I never would have considered before, and I continually seek new opportunities to grow and learn. Today, it is still a regular practice for me that if I am uncertain about my thoughts or feelings, I challenge them, listen to others, learn, make new decisions, and NEVER presume to know it all because there is always something new to learn. Sometimes that means we change our minds. When we do, we need to be mindful that this is not hypocrisy. It is evolution. Most importantly, I am no longer paralyzed by fear and anxiety.

I believe strongly in my ability to contribute to this world in a positive way. While it is not always easy to see things that have not come to fruition, I have experienced firsthand the successes of a wildly audacious imagination.

You see, when the desire to chase our dreams becomes more powerful than the lies our brains tell us, we find the courage to self-activate. Whether that means working on things within us or imagining something new and then making it become a reality, courage is the key to all the possibilities life has to offer. Instead of cowering from whatever worst-case scenario our anxious premonitions tell us we are doomed to experience, lean into discomfort. Learn to recognize that discomfort is not the enemy. Discomfort is life telling us that there is something new to learn, an opportunity to challenge our beliefs, maybe a new perspective to consider. This is where we invent, reinvent and grow.

If we can adjust our mindset to see discomfort as a welcomed opportunity, we begin to see that opportunity may be our next adventure. What's more, once we have tried it once or twice, and we have come out the other side relatively unscathed and a little wiser, we often recognize that it was not as painful as we imagined. And as I've discussed throughout this book, the point of this thing we call life is not to rush to the finish line, but to believe in yourself so much that you enjoy the trip there, and never regret a single moment. To be able to picture your wildest dreams and believe in yourself enough to make them come to fruition exists within all of us.

My wish for you is that I have given you some things to think about and a strategy to employ that will help you envision your wildest dreams—and that you find the courage to chase them. My hope for you is that through sharing my experiences, you will find the inspiration to love yourself so much that no matter what is happening outside you, you will always turn to the mirror to see a smile of love and self-assuredness reflected back at you.

Remember that sometimes hardship is inevitable, and it's okay to permit ourselves the joy of today, for if tomorrow never comes, worrying about things that have not yet happened will have been a waste of precious time. Instead, we can celebrate life knowing that we have done the best we can, acted with absolute integrity and honored ourselves by travelling the road to courageous living.

As for me, I am now in complete remission from leukemia and hope to be declared cured in December 2022. I make it a habit to appreciate my health, but never get overconfident because the reality is, all of us will experience health decline eventually. Marvin and I continue to prioritize making memories with our family, and I actively work towards checking off the boxes of all my dreams and non-negotiables because when I do finally leave this earth, I want to do it knowing I taught my children to live life to the absolute fullest.

ACKNOWLEDGMENTS

The journey of hitting the lowest point of my life, then recovery and the exponential growth that has occurred since has been terrifying, thrilling and more rewarding than I could ever have imagined. Through it all, my amazing husband, Marvin McDoom, has been by my side lifting me up and cheering me on every step of the way. I'm eternally grateful for his tenacity and patience through everything we have been through and everything that is to come.

A huge thank you to my kids, Victoria and Isabelle, who inspire me to be a better person every single day. Girls, your love and innocence remind me often of why I continue to do the hard work of unlearning, relearning, healing and growing. I love you both powerfully.

I'll never forget my father, stepmother and mother sitting together at the hospital, building the family plan of how they would support my family and me. My mother, Debbie Burleigh, stepped in to help manage day-to-day life through the most horrendous times when I was unable to function. Nor will I forget the sacrifice my stepmother, Daniela Burleigh, made when her husband left home for weeks to care for me in the hospital. Surely not to minimize the efforts of Gerry Burleigh, my father, as I was comforted by his presence during my days in the hospital, but what I am most grateful for was the day I called him from my car on my first solo road trip after finishing treatment. I told him I knew it was likely too soon for me to take a trip on my own, but I was compelled to go as the universe insisted I start my advocacy journey, and all he said in return was, "Honey, I understand." Thank you for believing in me, Dad.

A very special thank you to the nurses, doctors, technicians, administrative staff and porters who cared for me during my time at Juravinski Cancer Centre. Given the effort it took to make it to you, it is no small thing that you made me feel as safe as you did during my days with you. Your outstanding professionalism and compassion made a horrific experience a little more bearable than it otherwise might have been. A special mention to Kristine Leach, my nurse practitioner, whose expertise, kindness and humor is unparalleled. Beyond grateful for you.

I am acutely aware that I can talk any topic to death. An enormous thank you to all the people who listened to me rant incessantly while I worked through the life lessons described in this book and so much more. Their insights have led to some of the most pivotal shifts in my life and their friendship has taught me to love deeper, fight harder and dream bigger. Jessica Hall, Kristen Nembhard and Tuyen Dang, your wisdom is fiercely cherished.

Thank you to my psychotherapist, Natalie Hayes, who has always provided a safe, judgment-free zone to explore the scariest corners of my memory. Your guidance has helped me see life through a different lens which allowed me to leave the past in the past and made room for the possibilities that life has to offer.

Last, but certainly not least, thank you to all of the spectacular humans that have supported me through my recovery and the process of publishing my first book. Writing a book—self-publishing a book is no small feat, nor is cancer recovery, and to do so required an entire army. Huge thank yous to a long list of people, not limited to the following: Jennifer MacIntyre, Leigh

Carter, Lisa Poshni from Lisa Poshni Photography, Marvin McDoom from Virago DSigns, Courtney St Croix, and everyone who has supported me personally and the success of this project. A special thank you to Thie Convery from kicking me in the butt to get this project started!

RESOURCES AND REFERENCES

- Hamilton Health Sciences: https://www.hamiltonhealthsciences.ca/share/sepsis-canada/
- Advocis: www.advocis.ca
- American Society of Hematology: Volume 118, Issue 5, August 4, 2011, https://doi.org/10.1182/blood-2011-04-346437

GLOSSARY OF TERMS

Acute promyelocytic leukemia: Acute promyelocytic leukemia (APL) is a unique subtype of acute myeloid leukemia (AML) in which cells in the bone marrow that produce blood cells (red cells, white cells and platelets) do not develop and function normally.

Cold capping: Cold capping is a non-invasive, drug-free way of reducing hair loss after chemotherapy by cooling the scalp during treatment.

Hydromorphone: A drug used to treat moderate to severe pain. It may also be used to treat certain types of coughs. Hydromorphone hydrochloride is made from morphine and binds to opioid receptors in the central nervous system. It is a type of opioid and a type of analgesic agent.

Lymphatic System: is a network of delicate tubes throughout the body. It drains fluid (called lymph) that has leaked from the blood vessels into the tissues and empties it back into the bloodstream via the lymph nodes. The main roles of the lymphatic system include: managing the fluid levels in the body.

Melanoma: Melanoma is a form of skin cancer that begins in the cells (melanocytes) that control the pigment in your skin.

Meloxicam: Meloxicam is a nonsteroidal anti-inflammatory drug used to treat pain and inflammation in rheumatic diseases and osteoarthritis.

Mucositis: A complication of some cancer therapies in which the lining of the digestive system becomes inflamed. Often seen as sores in the mouth.

Narcotic: The term narcotic originally referred medically to any psychoactive compound with numbing or paralyzing properties. In the United States, it has since become associated with opiates and opioids, commonly morphine and heroin, as well as derivatives of many of the compounds found within raw opium latex.

Neutropenic: Neutropenia (noo-troe-PEE-nee-uh) occurs when you have too few neutrophils, a type of white blood cells. While all white blood cells help your body fight infections, neutrophils are important for fighting certain infections, especially those caused by bacteria.

Nonsteroidal anti-inflammatory drug (NSAID): Non-steroidal anti-inflammatory drugs are members of a therapeutic drug class which reduces pain, decreases inflammation, decreases fever, and prevents blood clots.

Peripherally inserted central catheter: A peripherally inserted central catheter (PICC), also called a PICC line, is a long, thin tube that's inserted through a vein in your arm and passed through to the larger veins near your heart.

Platelets: A tiny, disc-shaped piece of cell that is found in the blood and spleen. Platelets are pieces of very large cells in the bone marrow called megakaryocytes. They help form blood clots to slow or stop bleeding and to help wounds heal.

Telehealth Ontario: Telehealth Ontario was replaced in 2022 by the government of Ontario and Ontario Health. The new telephone service is called Health Connect Ontario.

*Some names have been changed to protect the identities of those people.

ABOUT THE AUTHOR

After recovering from an aggressive, life-threatening illness, Michelle Burleigh founded the Clarity Lab, an organization dedicated to improving the patient experience in the Canadian healthcare system. Michelle educates and inspires Canadians to take a proactive role in their own care and supports healthcare organizations in shifting towards patient-centric tools and solutions. She endeavours to have a meaningful, positive impact on the Canadian healthcare ecosystem by advocating for safe and exceptional patient experiences.

Stay connected to Michelle by signing up for notifications at www.soyouvegotcancer.ca and follow her on social media at:

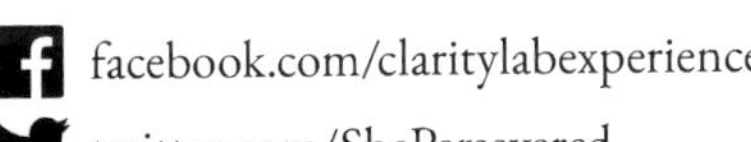

facebook.com/claritylabexperience
twitter.com/ShePersevered_
instagram.com/she_persevered_still
tiktok.com/@she_persevered

Manufactured by Amazon.ca
Bolton, ON

31232089R00083